Indian Public Management
Case Studies for Good Governance

About the Editors

B. Ashok, joined the IAS while undergoing research training in Biotechnology in IVRI, Uttar Pradesh in 1998. He is also an alumnus of London, Turin and Duke Universities in various postgraduate and research training programmes. Previously Deputy Director and Course Director in the Lal Bahadur Shastri National Academy of Administration, Mussoorie, Dr. Ashok had jointly won the best Indian Social Science Research Paper Award in 2009.

H.M. Mishra, a Ph.D. in Political Sociology and currently Professor of Sociology in RCVP Noronha Academy of Administration & Management, Bhopal and Chief Executive, Centre for Knowledge Management and Good Governance (CKMGG) established under Society Act, was Professor, Social Management in Lal Bahadur Shastri National Academy of Administration, Mussoorie, Uttarakhand.

Indian Public Management Case Studies for Good Governance

Editors
B. Ashok
H.M. Mishra

CONCEPT PUBLISHING COMPANY PVT. LTD.
NEW DELHI-110059

ISBN-13: 978-81-8069-877-4

First Published 2012

Published and Printed by

Concept Since 1974

Concept Publishing Company Pvt. Ltd.
A/15-16, Commercial Block, Mohan Garden
New Delhi-110059 (India)
T: 25351460, 25351794, *F*: 091-11-25357109
E: publishing@conceptpub.com, W: www.conceptpub.com
Editorial Office: H-13, Bali Nagar, New Delhi-110 015, India.

Cataloging in Publication Data--*Courtesy:* D.K. Agencies (P) Ltd. <docinfo@dkagencies.com>

Indian public management : case studies for good governance / editors, B. Ashok, H.M. Mishra.
p. cm.
Contributed articles.
Includes bibliographical references and index.
ISBN 9788180698774

1. Public administration—India—Case studies. 2. India—Politics and government. I. Ashok, B. II. Mishra, H. M.

DDC 351.54 23

Preface

The Case Study method appealed to the course team of the 2008 professional programme for IAS officers in the LBSNAA, Mussoorie and it was encouraged with academics and practitioners writing cases and delivering them to a very good reception. The method proved interactive, engaging and simulated learning by doing. Some cases cut across the need for which they were written and serve excellent discussion material towards larger issues in Law and Polity. If discussed they serve as valuable learning materials for courses in Law and Public Policy as well. When Concept expressed interest in this edited version we were overjoyed since these cases written for a limited audience were now being thrown open to a larger audience. Contacts of the writers are also provided if any institution would like to request the case discussion in any of their courses. We welcome criticism and suggestions.

Dr. B. Ashok
Prof. H.M. Mishra

Acknowledgements

This volume could have not been possible without the generous contributions and permission of the authors, the Directors of LBSNAA—Shri Rudhra Gangadharan and Padam Vir Singh—supporting the method and cases, Prof. Dr. H.M. Mishra is editing it up and my family in suffering in silence when they were being collected, written or being brushed up. Thanks are due to all initial participants in various courses who helped shape the matter. Thanks are due to Kim, my pet Labrador for my intense debates with her during long walks in Mussoorie where she participated with winks, wags and barks.

List of Contributors

Prasanth N. is an Indian Administrative Service (IAS) Officer of 2007 batch, born on Kerala cadre. Presently he is the Managing Director of Kerala Tourism Development Corporation. He was Assistant Collector (under training), Kozhikode at the time of writing the case study. He is presently working in Kerala.

Sanjeev Chopra an IAS Officer of the 1990 batch. He is presently Joint Director at the LBSNAA Mussoorie.

B. Ashok is an Indian Administrative Service (IAS) Officer, currently Private Secretary to the Minister of State for Agriculture. He served earlier on the Faculty of the Lal Bahadur Shastri National Academy of Administration (LBSNAA), Mussoorie. He was also a scholar in Peace and Conflict at the Turin University in Italy.

Darez Ahamed was Assistant Collector (under training) in Madurai, Tamil Nadu at the time of writing. The fieldwork was part of Darez's district assignment to the LBSNAA.

Contents

1

Case Study Methodology

Introduction

The case study method of teaching used in Public Policy and Management (PPM) education is quite different from most of the methods of teaching used at the school and undergraduate course levels. Unlike traditional lecture-based teaching where student participation in the classroom is unidirectional and minimal, the case method is an active learning method, which requires participation and involvement from the student in the classroom. For students who have been exposed only to the traditional teaching methods, this calls for a major change in their approach to learning. Without a paradigm shift from both instructors and learners and focus on pre-class intensive preparation, case method will not yield optimal results.

This collection of cases is intended to provide students with some basic instruments on the case method, and a few selected cases. We begin by taking a brief look at what case studies are, and how they are used in the classroom. Then we discuss what the student needs to do to prepare for a class, and what she can expect during the case discussion: We consider the benefits a student of PPM can expect to gain through the use of the case method.

What is a Case Study?

There is no universally accepted definition for a case study, and the case method means different things to different people. Consequently, all case studies are not structured similarly, and variations abound in terms of style, structure and approach. Case material ranges from small caselets (a few paragraphs to one or two pages) to short cases (four to six pages) and from 10 to 18 page case studies to the longer versions (25 pages and above).

A case is usually a "description of an actual situation, commonly involving a decision, a challenge, an opportunity, a problem or an issue faced by a person or persons in an organization. In learning with case studies, the student must deal with the situation described in the case, in the role of the manager or decision maker facing the situation.

Multiplicity of Solutions

An important point to be emphasized here is that a case is not a problem. A problem usually has a unique, correct solution. On the other hand, a decision-maker faced with the situation described in a case can choose between several alternative courses of action, and each of these alternatives may plausibly be supported by logical argument. To put it simply, there is no unique, correct answer in the case study method.

The case study method usually involves three stages: individual preparation, small group discussion, and large group or class discussion. While both the instructor and the student start with the same information, their roles are clearly different in each of these stages.

Case Studies in the Classroom

Case studies are usually discussed in class, in a plenary group. However, sometimes, instructors may require individuals or groups of students to provide a written analysis of a case study which may or may not be graded, or make an oral presentation on the case study in the classroom.

Preparing for a Case Discussion

Unlike lecture-based teaching, the case method requires intensive preparation by the students, before each class. If a case has been assigned for discussion in the class, the student must prepare carefully and thoroughly for the case discussion. It is ideal if the case study discussion class is preceded by a reading recess.

The first step in this preparation is to read the case thoroughly. To grasp the situation described in a case study, the student will need to read it several times. The first reading of the case can be a light one, to get a broad idea of the story. The subsequent readings must be more focused, to help the student become familiar with the facts of the case, and the issues that are important in the situation being described in the case — the who, what, where, why and how of the case.

However, familiarity with the facts described in the case is not enough. If necessary the student must also acquire a thorough understanding of the case situation, through a detailed analysis of the case using secondary web/library resources. During the case analysis process, the student must attempt to identify the main protagonists in the case study (organizations, groups, or individuals described in the case) and their relationships.

The student must also keep in mind that in the different kinds of information are presented in the case study. There are facts, which are verifiable from several sources. There are inferences, which represent an individual's judgment in a given situation. There is speculation, which is information which cannot be verified. There are also assumptions, which cannot be verified, and are generated during case analysis or discussion. Clearly, all these different types of information are not equally valuable for decision-making. Usually, the greater your reliance on facts (rather than speculation or assumptions), the better the logic and persuasiveness of your arguments and the quality of your decisions. Sometimes data is over supplied to confuse the student. A careful selection of facts to be used to take decisions is also crucial.

Broadly speaking, the different stages in the case analysis process could be as follows:

1. Gaining familiarity with the case situation (critical case facts, persons, activities, contexts);
2. Recognizing the symptoms (what are the things that are not as expected, or as they should be?);

3. Identifying goals/objectives;
4. Conducting the analysis;
5. Making the diagnosis (identifying problems, i.e. discrepancies between goals and performance, prioritizing problems, etc.);
6. Preparing the action plan (identifying feasible action alternatives, selecting a course of action, implementation planning, plan for monitoring implementation).

Case Discussions in the Classroom

A classroom case discussion is usually guided by the instructor. Students are expected to participate in the discussion and present their views. In some cases, the instructor may adopt a particular view, and challenge the students to respond. During the discussion, while a student presents his point of view, others may question or challenge him. Case instructors usually encourage innovative ways of looking at and analyzing problems, and arriving at possible alternatives. The idea is to develop multiple narratives and conflicting view points of the same set of facts.

The interaction among students, and between the students and the instructor, must take place in a constructive and positive manner. Such interactions help to improve the analytical, communication, and interpersonal skills of the students. However, some control has to be exercised to focus on the pre-identified core issues especially in the latter 40 per cent of time allotted use of Flip charts and white boards to post the "Core issues" is ideal to focus discussion.

Students must be careful that the contributions they make to the discussion are relevant, and based on a sound analysis of the information presented in the case. Students can also refer to the notes they have prepared during the course of their preparation for the case discussion. While open humorous phases are welcome initially, one will have to focus on learning points sooner or later. Case study needs excellent and control capability of instructors.

The instructor may ask questions to the class at random about the case study itself or about the views put forward by an individual student. If a student has some new insights about the issues at hand, she is usually encouraged to share them with the class.

Students must respond when the instructor asks some pertinent questions. The importance of preparing beforehand cannot be emphasized enough — a student will be able to participate meaningfully in the case discussion only if he is knowledgeable about the facts of the case, and has done a systematic case analysis. A case discussion may end with the instructor (or a student) summarizing the key learning points (or 'takeaways') of the session. Many instructions circulate, after a first round of discussion 'a pre-prepared' points for discussion.

Student performance in case discussions is usually evaluated, and is a significant factor in assessing overall performance in the course. The extent of participation is never the sole criterion in the evaluation — the quality of the participation is an equally (or more) important criterion. The ability to ask pointed questions and 'deepen the debate' is a key criteria while evaluating student performance.

Working in a Group

If a group of students is asked to analyze a case, they must ensure that they meet to discuss and analyze the case, by getting together for a group meeting at a suitable time and location. Before the meeting, all the team members must read the case and come with their own set of remarks/observations.

The group must ensure that all the group members contribute to the preparation and discussion. It is important that the group is able to work as a cohesive team — problems between team members are likely to have an adverse impact on the group's overall performance.

Preparing a Written Case Analysis

Quite often, a written analysis of the case may be a part of the internal evaluation process. When a written analysis of a case is required, the student must ensure that the analysis is properly structured.

An instructor may provide specific guidelines about how the analysis is to be structured. However, when submitting an analysis, the student must ensure that it is neat and free from any factual, language and grammar errors. In fact, this is a requirement for any report that a student may submit — not just a case analysis. Most courses will require this to be in work procured or excel format.

Making a Case Presentation

The instructor may ask a group of students to present their analysis and recommendations to the class. Alternatively, an individual student can also be asked to make a presentation.

The key to a good presentation is good preparation. If the case has been studied and analyzed thoroughly, the content of the presentation should present no problems.

However, a presentation is more than the content. Some of the points that need to be kept in mind when making a case presentation are:

- As far as possible, divide the content uniformly so that each team member gets an opportunity to speak.
- Use visual aids such as OHP slides, Power Point presentations, advertisement/press clippings etc., as much as possible to advance the agreement.
- Be brief and to-the-point. Stick to the time limits set by the instructor. Do not allow a few participants to monopolize the discussion. Set ground rules that participants do not speak for more than 2 minutes at a speech.
- Be well prepared.

Evaluating Student Performance

The evaluation of a student's performance in a case-driven course can be based on some or all of the following factors:

- Written case analyses (logical flow and structuring of the content, language and presentation, quality of analysis and recommendations, etc.).
- Case presentations (communication skills, logical flow and structuring of the content, quality of analysis and recommendations, etc.).
- Participation in classroom case discussions (quality and extent of participation).
- Case writing assignments or similar projects.
- Case-based examinations.

Benefits from the Case Method

The case method has several advantages over traditional teaching methods. The skills that students develop by being exposed to this method are many and are described below. The consequences to the student from involvement in the method are listed thereafter.

- Cases allow students to learn by doing. They allow students to step into the shoes of decision-makers in real organizations, and deal with the issues public managers face, with no risk to themselves or the organization involved.
- Cases improve the students ability to ask the right questions, in a given problem situation. Their ability to identify and understand the underlying problems rather than the symptoms of the problems is also enhanced.
- Case studies expose student's to a wide range of industries, organizations, functions and responsibility levels. This provides students the flexibility and confidence to deal with a variety of tasks and responsibilities in their careers. It also helps students to make more informed decisions about their career choices.

Results of Case Based Learning

- Cases studies strengthen the student's grasp of management theory, by providing real-life examples of the underlying theoretical concepts. By providing rich, interesting information about real business situations, they breathe life into conceptual discussions.
- Cases provide students with an exposure to the actual working of business and other organizations in the real world.
- Case studies reflect the reality of managerial decision-making in the real world, in that students must make decisions based on insufficient information. Cases reflect the ambiguity and complexity that accompany most management issues.
- When working on a case study in a group, students must also be able to understand and deal with the different viewpoints and perspectives of the other members in their

team. This serves to improve their communication and interpersonal skills.

- Case studies provide an integrated view of management. Managerial decision-making involves integration of theories and concepts learnt in different functional areas such as marketing and finance. The case method exposes students to this reality of management.

Source: 1993, C.C. Lundberg and C. Enz, 'A Framework for Student Case Preparation', *Case Research Journal*, 13 (Summer) 134/Michael A. Hitt, R. Duane Ireland and Robert E. Hoskisson, Strategic Management (Thomson Southwestern, 6th Edition) Cii as adapted.

2

Case for Discussion

Barring the Bar Dancers

B. Ashok

The State Government of Maharashtra (GoM) in India, after a brief discussion in the State Assembly (Legislature) passed the Mumbai Police Amendment Bill (2005) in August 2005, imposing a ban on any type of dance performances in legal places, eating places, permit rooms and beer bars selling alcohol. The law exempted hotels above three star rating, theatres and sports clubs from the purview of the ban for tourism purposes.

The ban was aimed at prohibiting dancing in beer/liquor parlours which were previously licensed for Mumbai and other cities. Under State licences which came for a very hefty fee, the bars were permitted to have dancers perform in the stage, under supervision from local police. The patrons were not allowed to dance with the dancers (usually female) or contact them physically. The patrons, usually males relaxing after work, or teenagers experimenting with the secrets of life, comprising of rich and poor and young and mature alike, showered currency notes on individual dancers which was later shared between the dancers and the bar owner.

The provocation for the ban came from various anti-dance bar groups who petitioned the GoM against them, some petitions having up to 15,000 signatures. Assertions by the State Deputy Chief Minister Mr. R.R. Patil, who argued that the dance bars are "dens of criminal activity and places where law enforcement officials and criminals met and struck deals" were sought to legitimize the ban.

Leading the case for the Government, he argued that the dance bars are a blot on the morals of the Mumbai society and a corrupting influence on the youth. The Government also had evidence that many rival bar owners used illegal means including violation of the licensing conditions (allowing patrons to dance along or provide secret retiring rooms where patrons could have sex with the dancers) to further the commerce. Many reputed public persons and rival bar owners had in fact complained to the existence of such malpractices. Raids on several bars had also revealed such practices; the owners of those were being prosecuted.

The Maharashtra Assembly was unanimous in passing the legislation and there was absolutely no discussion pointing to any undesirability on the government move. There was unanimity in the Assembly on the view that the working of the dance bars was a threat to public order and safety from the case the government argued on the floor of the house. Not only that speaker after speaker condemned the bar dancers and their immoral influence on the society, very derogatory remarks were made on them, one member even describing them as polluters of the Indian family ethos and values. Comments made on the floor of the House included: "Isha Koppikar. . . . she is an atom bomb, atom bomb. . . . This evoked great deal of laughter and cheer. . . . "The dancers wear only 20 per cent clothes". . . . More laughter and cheering. . . . "These women who dance naked (*nanga nach*), they do not deserve any sympathy".

One member narrated an incident of his friend's daughter who had committed suicide because she did not get a job. He said it was more dignified to commit suicide than dance in bars. And the House applauded ! Yet another congratulated the Deputy Home Minister for taking this bold and revolutionary step, but this was not enough. He urged that "hotels with three stars. . . . five stars, disco dancing. . . . belly dancing. . . . all that is vulgar. . . . everything should be banned, except *Bharatnatyam* and *Kathak*. (Indian classical dances.)"

How will the State effect this ban, when through its own admission out of around 1300 dance bars only 307 are legal and authorized? Legislators opined that Western, English and Tamil films are all obscene. But they did not say a word about Hindi and Marathi films presumably because these belong to "*amchi Mumbai*".

Invoking of the ban threw, according to NGOs, 75,000 to 100,000 dancers and associated workers like bouncers, waiters, cashiers, cleaners, auto-taxi drivers etc., out of work causing a serious socio-economic repercussion in Mumbai. Not only that the out of work bar dancers formed the "Bhartiya Bar Dancing Girls Union", and along with the bar owners association challenged the Government order in the High Court of Mumbai. They also formed a popular movement which contested civic polls without much success but received high degree of support from performing artistes and civil society. Media also, generally championed their cause.

The bar dancers are mostly from poorer neighbouring States of Maharashtra and come to the city after suffering abject deprivation or lack of any worthwhile future in their own small towns or villages. A typical dancer from Uttar Pradesh, who was abandoned by her husband, revealed that she earned Rs. 15,000 per month (or Rs. 500 per night) of dancing. Suddenly depriving 75,000 such destitute dancers of legitimate income (since government licensed such activity) would have serious social repercussions. For instance, many of the agitating bar dancers pointed out that they had no other option now but to turn to clandestine prostitution. Within three months of the Mumbai ban three types of related crimes were being reported.

One was the migration and clandestine dancing in cities like Delhi and Bangalore, where opportunistic middle men and entertainers were hiring unemployed Mumbai girls to dance in riskier circumstances —like private hotel rooms. Some sting operations by media revealed girls being forced to dance vulgar or nude. Second was an increase in prostitution within Mumbai city with so many young women suddenly out of work. A third was springing up of illegal dance bars in suburban Mumbai where the police had no ready information. Wealthy clients were arranging mujras, etc., in private farm houses, etc. There was, clearly, a market for dancing and it would not just go away overnight. Over 25 bar dancers were reported to have committed suicide in the period of the ban.

The legal challenge to the ban on bar dancing has been led by civil society lawyers. They point out that the ban is violative of the right to life and work enshrined in the Constitution (Article 21) and the right to pursue a legitimate profession (Article 19). Dancing broadly falls under the fundamental rights guaranteed in the Constitution of India in the right of speech and expression (Article 19).

In support of the bar girls cause, it was maintained that the standard Bollywood Hindi films carried more vulgar dance sequences which were beamed right into family audiences by cable operators. In the peak of the ban controversy the Maharashtra Police organized a dance show where a celebrity dancer was alleged to have performed with far lesser attire than an average bar dancer. Live telecasts of New Year's Eve celebrations of Mumbai's premier starred hotels also showed that the bar girls' dance was much less lewd in comparison. The only difference was the high end hotels catered to the glitterati while the low end bar dancers catered to the lower middle working class.

The Maharashtra initiative was not isolated since it came in a series of control measures started at the time of the previous regime. Though they opposed the ban, during their time in power, the opposition had also sought to control the entertainment industry.

Protests were organized especially by middle class activists including women, against the revoking of the ban. The ban had a positive impact on the middle class who were wary of hurt to the value system and the moral damage the bars were causing. According to them, enticed men got lured away and spent their entire earnings in dance bars while hundreds of families were destituted. They cited cases where young bright boys got infected with HIV in dance bar liaisons and men who got addicted to dancers, drinks or drugs blowing up their entire savings. They felt that the ban would reduce neighbourhood crime and drunken disorderly behaviour and improve traffic. Police sources also point to the regulatory thrust on them burden is lower after the ban since they do not have to attend drunken brawls, etc.

The social activists and actors including leading MPs like Mr. Sunil Dutt protested the ban since they felt that it was the act of an over arching patriarchal State, more than the deprivation of the bar dancers. Many activists contend that the dancing tradition is nothing new to Mumbai. In fact *mujra, lavni* and *tamasha* dancing were legitimate entertainment in many parts of North India. Such semi-lewd portrayal and the status of such dancers were protected in the social system. The tradition is further underlined by the fact of ritual dancers and dancing/prostitution tribes and castes in some parts of India. In the South also there is a tradition of ritual prostitution with girls being devoted as *'yellamma'* or *'devadasis'*. This is on the wane after social activists and governments are rehabilitating the tradition bound castes.

The more extreme amongst the activists would argue that prostitution itself must be licensed and protected since absolute destitution is worse than a woman being able to take care of her and family by resorting to selling her only possession: her body. In the absence of an effective protective State which has failed to provide either education or skills, she has to be permitted to defend life with whatever capital she possesses. They would argue for protective legislation as in Netherlands, recognizing licensed areas for prostitution, regular medical check ups and safety from the law enforces who abuse them in every possible manner.

Surveys amongst sex workers reveal that they are routinely abused by constabulary, who seek sex with them often without payment; extract *hafta* (protection money) and also impart physical abuses and false up on cases on refusal. Known to be prostitutes, they are often refused medical screening or care and many are carriers of STDs and HIV. Non-regulated prostitution, they feel, is the problem than prostitution *per se*.

The activists would pose this question to the supporters of the ban: If parts of the dance club system were indeed violating the law, would it mean that the State can shut the entire livelihood down? If some officers are corrupt does it shut the *Mantralaya* down? Can the State play moral police on an individual's freedom to have entertainment? Is it not against fundamental rights and discriminatory to deprive the choice of entertainment in a dance bar when the same is available through other licensed popular media? Is it feasible in the age of openness, permissiveness, internet and exposure to ban a few dance bars and get high on morality? In case the government argues for public order should it not ban consumption of liquor and even *paan* and cigarettes? Do the public and *netas* always conform to such chaste behaviour? The NGOs documented the Maharashtra Police resorting to entertaining dancers for its annual welfare fund collection and leading State politicians patronizing *mujra* dancers.

Government claims that only 11,000 dancing girls are involved in the ban and all other estimates by NGOs are false and concocted. Comparisons were made with the nexus between crime and dance bars where a noted criminal fraudster, one Abdul Karim Telgi who presided over a huge financial scam showered Rs. one crore on a famous dancer of that time in just one night. Such showering of currency was, some psychologists argue, addictive and difficult to get rid of. One Sri Lankan cricketer was known to patronize one particular dancer and even got personal performances arranged.

The case was simultaneously before the High Court of Bombay and the public.

In the mean time the future of 75,000 bar dancers hang in balance.

- *Discuss the constitutional rights in conflict here and give your personal argument in favour of or against the ban on bar dancing legislated in Mumbai by GOM?*
- *What other alternatives were available to the GOM to reduce ill effects of bar dancing?*

RELEVANT PROVISIONS OF THE CONSTITUTION OF INDIA

Right to Freedom

Article 19. Protection of certain rights regarding freedom of speech, etc.—(1) All citizens shall have the right—

(a) to freedom of speech and expression;
(b) to assemble peaceably and without arms;
(c) to form associations or unions;
(d) to move freely throughout the territory of India;
(e) to reside and settle in any part of the territory of India;
Article 13 [and]
Article 14* * * * *
(g) to practise any profession, or to carry on any occupation, trade or business.

Article 15[(2) Nothing in sub-clause (a) of clause (1) shall affect the operation of any existing law, or prevent the State from making any law, in so far as such law imposes reasonable restrictions on the exercise of the right conferred by the said sub-clause in the interests of Article 16 [the sovereignty and integrity of India,] the security of the State, friendly relations with foreign States, public order, decency or morality, or in relation to contempt of court, defamation or incitement to an offence.]

(3) Nothing in sub-clause (b) of the said clause shall affect the operation of any existing law in so far as it imposes, or prevents the State from making any law imposing, in the interests of Article 16 [the sovereignty and integrity of India or] public order, reasonable restrictions on the exercise of the right conferred by the said sub-clause.

(4) Nothing in sub-clause (c) of the said clause shall affect the operation of any existing law in so far as it imposes, or prevents the State from making any law imposing, in the interests of Article 16 [the sovereignty and integrity of India or] public order or morality, reasonable restrictions on the exercise of the right conferred by the said sub-clause.

(5) Nothing in Article 17 [sub-clauses (d) and (e)] of the said clause shall affect the operation of any existing law in so far as it imposes, or prevents the State from making any law imposing, reasonable restrictions on the exercise of any of the rights conferred by the said sub-clauses either in the interests of the general public or for the protection of the interests of any Scheduled Tribe.

(6) Nothing in sub-clause (g) of the said clause shall affect the operation of any existing law in so far as it imposes or prevents the State from making any law imposing, in the interests of the general public, reasonable restrictions on the exercise of the right conferred by the said sub-clause, and, in particular, Article18 [nothing in the said sub-clause shall affect the operation of any existing law in so far as it relates to, or prevent the State from making any law relating to,—

(i) the professional or technical qualifications necessary for practising any profession or carrying on any occupation, trade or business, or

(ii) the carrying on by the State, or by a corporation owned or controlled by the State, of any trade, business, industry or service, whether to the exclusion, complete or partial, of citizens or otherwise].

Article 21. Protection of life and personal liberty.—No person shall be deprived of his life or personal liberty except according to procedure established by law.

Right against Exploitation

Article 23. Prohibition of traffic in human beings and forced labour.—(1) Traffic in human beings and *begar* and other similar forms of forced labour are prohibited and any contravention of this provision shall be an offence punishable in accordance with law.

(2) Nothing in this article shall prevent the State from imposing compulsory service for public purposes, and in imposing such service the State shall not make any discrimination on grounds only of religion, race, caste or class or any of them.

33 Per cent Bar Girls Support Ban: Government (Various Press Reports)

The dance bar ban has been popular among those whom it has hit the hardest—the bar dancers—the State government has claimed. It told the Bombay High Court on Thursday that according to a recent study conducted among 72 women working in bars, 33 per cent of them supported the ban, 25 per cent wanted it to be revoked and 42 per cent did not respond.

The State was quoting from a study by Prayas, a Tata Institute of Social Sciences (TISS) project, to justify the ban on dance bars. However, according to the petitioners opposing the ban, the Prayas report, which was prepared after the government announced the ban, has "glaring problems of methodology and ethical issues". In fact, one of the petitioners, the Forum Against Oppression of Women (FAOW), has written to TISS pointing out the glitches. Quoting the report, Advocate General Ravi Kadam said that 6 per cent of the 72 girls interviewed were minors while 87 per cent fell in the age group of 18 to 30 years. As many as 50 per cent were illiterate, 13 per cent had studied up to standard 4, 17 per cent between standards 5 and 10 and only 1 per cent were graduates.

According to the study, 47 per cent of the girls interviewed were ashamed of their work and had not told their families about where they worked. The study pegged their earnings at Rs. 50 to Rs. 500 per day of which bar owners claimed 30 to 60 per cent. Picking holes in the Prayas study, which played an active role in getting the ban enacted, the FAOW letter to TISS states in the sample size of 72 women working in bars, 57 per cent were dancers, 26 per cent worked as waitresses and for 17 per cent "no information is available". In effect, the researchers spoke to 35 dancers, which is "highly inadequate" when the issue affects 75,000 bar dancers, the letter said.

Socio-economic Situation and Rehabilitation Needs of Women in Dance Bars

Sample size : 72 women working in bars (57% bar dancers, 26% waitresses, 17 % no information available)

Reactions to the ban: 33 per cent supported the ban, 25 per cent opposed the ban, 42 per cent No reaction

Age : 6 per cent below 6 years; 87 per cent 18 to 30 years; 6 per cent 31 to 40 years; 1 per cent not known

Education : 50 per cent Illiterate; 13 per cent Class IV; 17 per cent Class V to X; 1 per cent HSC; 1 per cent Graduation; 18 per cent No information

Marital status : 68 per cent married; 21 per cent unmarried; 1 per cent not known. 47 per cent of the married women were either deserted, divorced or widows; 71 per cent had children to support

Whether family knows about their profession : 21 per cent family aware; 47 per cent family unaware; 32 per cent No

(*According to the Prayas Study*)

THE HIGH COURT RAISES THE BAR

Ban on Dance Bars is Discriminatory since it does not apply to Hotels and Clubs

Government Order curbs Right to Livelihood of Bar Girls and Owners, says Court

Mumbai: In a major embarrassment to the Democratic Front

government and its Deputy Chief Minister R.R. Patil, the Bombay High Court on Wednesday struck down the State Government's law banning dance bars.

The Court, in a 260-page ruling, held that the law was void as it imposed "an unreasonable restriction" which was "not in the public interest". The ban, enforced from August 15 last year on grounds of "immorality and obscenity", was touted as one of the key achievements of the Congress-NCP alliance.

A division bench of Justice F.I. Rebello and Justice Roshan Dalvi, hearing a bunch of public interest petitions by bar owners, bar girls, activists and NGOs challenging the government legislation, ruled that the ban violated the fundamental rights and constitutional right to equality of bar dancers and bar owners.

While the judges maintained that the law "did not violate the dancers' or bar owners' right to life or freedom of speech and expression", as claimed by the petitioners, they took exception to the fact that the State government was restricting dance performances only in dance bars, restaurants and permit rooms, while allowing hotels, clubs and discotheques to continue with these. They said that the blanket ban on all types of dances in these places did not have any connection with the object of the ban which, according to the government, was "to prevent dances which are obscene, vulgar or immoral and derogatory to the dignity of women".

The judges said that the government's justification for the ban on the grounds that the bar girls were exploited did not stand the test. "If women other than dancers can work in prohibited establishments and that does not amount to exploitation, we do not see why, when women dance to earn their livelihood, it becomes exploitation", said the judges.

As celebrations erupted outside the court, Advocate General Ravi Kadam said the State would challenge the order in the Apex Court.

Despite Wednesday's orders, dance bars will not be able to re-open for at least eight weeks, as the performance licences of all bars were cancelled following the ban. Although the High Court rejected the State government's application for a stay on the order, it said that performance licences would be issued only after eight weeks. This interval will allow the State to prepare its appeal in the Apex Court.

Now that the Bombay High Court has lifted the ban on dance bars once again, voices decrying obscenity in these establishments are bound to come to the fore again. The police, however, will have to be careful before they *suo motu* brand a dance as obscene and act against it. This too is an outcome of previous High Court judgments.

In the past, cops have often booked dancers and bar owners, and sometimes even patrons, under Section 294 of the Indian Penal Code (IPC) which pertains to "obscene acts and songs".

"Bar premises would be raided by the police and owners booked," says lawyer Vina Thadani.

"However, the section requires that a person watching a particular programme is annoyed or offended by it and makes a complaint to the police", she added. In 2004 Justices Ranjana Desai and P.V. Kakade had clarified that the police could not act on their own account.

- ❑ *August 15:* Ban comes into effect across Maharashtra.
- ❑ *October:* Multiple petitions lodged in Bombay High Court against ban.
- ❑ *April 12, 2006:* High Court overturns government ban.

Figures that Matter

- ❑ *No of bar girls:* 1 lakh
- ❑ *No of bars:* 1250
- ❑ *Average Earning of a Bar Girl:* Rs. 500/night
- ❑ *No. of girls who committed suicide between August 2005 and April 2006:* 25

Government Gets 8 Weeks to File Appeal

The High Court also gave a clean chit to Deputy C.M. R.R. Patil, against whom the bar owners had made allegations of bribery. There was no *prima facie* evidence for these claims, the judges said. The Court has, however, directed Police Commissioner A.N. Roy to investigate allegations that two party workers were dealing with Manjit Singh Sethi to "get the law amended for change in the timings of dance bars for a huge consideration". Roy has been asked to submit the report of the probe within three months.

Roy, who vigorously went after dance bars, was non-committal. "We have not received the judgment copy so far. The High Court has given eight weeks' time. During this period we will consider the next step on the basis of legal advice", he said.

In a bid to halt the entry of minors into the trade, Justice Roshan Dalvi, in a supplementary order, directed NGOs Prayas of the **Tata Institute of Social Sciences** and the Research Centre for Women's Studies of SNDT to conduct periodic inquiries into the dance bars to check trafficking of women, especially minors. In the event of such cases being found, the NGOs have been asked to report them to the nearest police station and arrange for the rescue and the rehabilitation of the children. The judge also recorded an assurance by the bar owners that they would never permit a single child to be abused in their premises.

Dozens of bar owners waited outside the Bombay High Court with bated breath for the judgment. As soon as it was clear that the court had ordered the ban to be lifted, the men started sending frantic SMSes and hugging each other.

Setback for Deputy C.M. R.R. Patil

Deputy Chief Minister R.R. Patil found himself a lonely man on Wednesday as the Bombay High Court overturned the ban on dance bars. Mantralaya insiders insist that Patil, to start with, was not opposed to the bars, but was forced to take a stand after several MLAs from rural Maharashtra complained about the adverse impact the bars were having on village youths. But the Deputy Chief Minister is now paying for identifying too closely with the ban.

MLAs send Bar Chief to Jail

The assembly on Wednesday handed out a 90-day jail term to Manjeet Singh Sethi, President of the Bar and Hotel Owners' Association, for alleged breach of privilege of the House. The verdict preceded the HC order by a few minutes. Sethi, who owns a dance bar in Dadar, was in the forefront of the campaign to oppose the ban and had threatened that bar girls would take to the streets and not allow the wives of ministers to move about freely.

Legal Provisions in the Case of the Bar Dancers

No.	Statute/Section	Wording/Effect	Remarks
1.	Constitution of India. COI A-13 (2)	State barred from any law against the rights (p-III) portion of the Constitution.	MPA bill 2005: whether violates existing rights in COI?
2.	COI A-14	Equality before law and equal protection of laws within territory.	Did MPA bill 2005 adhere to this?
3.	COI A-19 (a)	Freedom of speech and expression.	Dancing is a form of expression.
4.	COI A-19 (b)	Assemble peacefully without arms.	Bar dancing clubs are peaceful (?) associations.
5.	COI A-19 (g)/6	Freedom of profession, occupation, trade or business.	Dancing is entertainment business.
6.	COI A-21	Protection of life and liberty.	Includes right to livelihood.
7.	COI A-23	Right against trafficking in human beings and forced labour.	Attracted
8.	COI A 39 (a) (d)	Direct policy for securing livelihood Pay parity between sexes.	Attracted
9.	COI A 42	Just and humane conditions of work and maternity benefits.	Attracted
10.	COI A 46	Promotion of economic interests of SCs, STs and weaker sections.	Attracted
11.	IPC S-268	Public health convenience decay and morals/public nuisance.	Attracted
12.	Indian Penal Code. IPC S-269	Negligent act likely to spread disease.	Attracted

(Contd.)

No.	Statute/Section	Wording/Effect	Remarks
13.	IPC S-270	Malignant act likely to spread disease.	Attracted
14.	IPC Ss 372, 373	Kidnapping, forced slavery, etc.	Attracted
15.	IPC S 377	Un-natural offences	Attracted
16.	Immoral Trafficking. ITPA 1956/1986	Defines prostitution Women under 21 to remand homes. 1986 Expanded definition 3 Age categories procuring an offence 6 (4) No suit against the victim Identity to be protected	Attracted
17.	Criminal Procedure Code. Cr PC S-98/99	S-7: scope not near public places (200 metres) S-8: solicitation is offence S-20: Removal of prostitute from area Search for abducted female	Attracted

3

Crime, Punishment and Redemption?

B. Ashok

Introduction

The striking case of Mr. ABC, a convict-aspirant for the prestigious Union Public Service Commission's Civil Service Examinations conducted in 2007 has drawn media glare and raised a series of complicated questions regarding the implementation and theory of penal law and justice in the country. At the same time his experience which awaits adjudication at the highest appellate court of the country involves deep questions in public policy and also the social implication of conviction or acquittal in various crimes. A brief consideration of the circumstances in which Mr. ABC's case came to discussion is traced first to provoke a debate and raise some questions later.

Justice at Loggerheads

On 3rd April, 2008, Justices K. Balakrishnan and Sathasivam of the Indian Supreme Court observed in open court on the grounds upon which a lower provincial Delhi High Court had reduced and ordered the release of Mr. ABC a convict incarcerated in Delhi's Tihar Jail rather curtly: "It is not a relevant consideration. It will send a wrong signal. We do not agree with the reasons of the High Court."

The Justices set aside, temporarily, the Delhi High Court's division bench's verdict reducing Mr. ABC's conviction for abetment to suicide *vide* Section 306 IPC of his own tuition student Sushmita (an *alias*), aged 21, back in 2003. Sushmita, a student of Chemistry was receiving tuitions at Mr. ABC's classes when he presumably seduced her.

They had a relationship over an year in which they had, as per evidence before trial court, regular sexual intercourse. Later the deceased Sushmita and the prosecution, citing the evidence she left would claim in the trial court that Mr. ABC had first raped her under some intoxication and then threatened her with exposure if she did not cooperate every time he desired her sexually.

Mr. ABC's defence lawyers in the trial court had argued and maintain that there was indeed a consensual adult relationship involving sexual exchanges between them. They had cited evidence of the victim Sushmita taking contraceptive pills over a long period during which they were having sex.

The defence had argued unsuccessfully in the trial court that these were indicative of a consensual relationship, and the fact that the victim was aged 21, well past the legal age of consent (16 years) and never chose to withdraw or intimate authority or her own parents during the course of the relationship were drawn to the attention of the trial court and later the appellate superior Delhi High Court.

The prosecution, however, had the first taste of success with the trial court finding Mr. ABC guilty of Section 306 IPC and punished him with maximum punishment under the section, imprisonment for 10 years. Mr. ABC had started serving his life term in Delhi's Tihar Jail and his appeals on his trial court verdict were not favourable till 2009.

For a convict serving under extremely humiliating and stressing punishment Mr. ABC showed extraordinary will power, merit and determination when, after about five years of incarceration, he successfully competed for the UPSC's examination and qualified for being appointed as an IAS officer. If the Government of India would pardon him and appoint him, after release from jail, he would in a few years be in charge of the criminal administration of an entire district responsible for implementation of all laws preventing and trying offences against women including eve teasing and harassment. Later he could rise to become the Home Secretary of a State or even the Central Government responsible for all policy matters in the criminal justice sector amongst other things.

At this point Mr. ABC approached the High Court of Delhi which attracted the Court's sympathy.

In March 2009, as Mr. ABC's case was before the Government for appointment, the Delhi High Court speaking through Justices Pradeep Nandrajog and Aruna Suresh (lady) found sufficient grounds to commute Mr. ABC's sentence to the five and half years already served, from the ten he had to, and treat him 'redeemed' without clean acquittal as he had served enough time.

The High Court's Grounds

The violent disapproval of the Supreme Court cited here later was hinged on the fallacy of the reasoning that seems to have appealed to the High Court. The High Court had found reason to be clement to the convict on the following grounds:

He had persevered well under incarceration and had been studious enough to clear arguably a very tough entrance examination for Public Service. The fact that he qualified enough to be in the IAS, one of the most coveted jobs in the country sought after by bright graduates, showed his intention to be of use to society. These factors went favourably for a lenient consideration.

The High Court found also weaknesses in the evidence the trial court relied heavily on: that reliance of the dying declaration of the victim did not corroborate well with the rest of the evidence on the case made before the trial Court. The High Court felt that the imprisonment already undergone met the 'ends of justice', as he seemed to be only guilty of obtaining the victim's consent under a false promise. Other evidence pointed to the victim fully collaborating with the accused in a long drawn out sexual relationship.

At best Mr. ABC could be guilty of cheating and misrepresenting with criminal intent but there was hardly evidence of that alone pushing the victim to the extent of commit suicide. Statutorily that would constitute rape but the court was convinced that that alone did not push her to commit suicide. The victim had, clearly, overlooked other recourse for justice.

The court was critical of the victim for her participation and role in the crime. It observed: "At the age of 21 Sushmita was mature enough to understand the moral worth of her acts. She was conscious that by having repeated sex with ABC she could become pregnant and hence he had told her to take contraceptive pills. . . .There is some participative act committed by Sushmita. Therefore, her blaming ABC alone for her suicide does not hold water. . ."

Most of the prosecution rested, in the trial court on Sushmita's suicide note. She had held Mr. ABC responsible and narrated her suicide as being provoked by Mr. ABC's refusal to finally own up their indiscretion and marry her.

Amongst other things which dealt with cruel treatment and forced sexual acts, the suicide note also mentioned the fact that Sushmita lost all hope of a settlement when ABC threatened her with exposure if she did not have sex with a benefactor of his. It was her conflict of being in love with him and the pain of being exploited in the worst possible fashion that led her to commit suicide. The High Court, however, found no evidence supporting Sushmita's claims to this attempted "forced prostitution" as claimed in the suicide note.

In summary the High Court took the convict's demonstrated intentions to reform under incarceration and noted the weaknesses in the solid evidence against Mr. ABC while deciding favourably on his appeal. Legally the action of the High Court was fully within its ambit. It had perfect appellate jurisdiction and was acting within its constitutional powers. It may be mentioned here that the Government of Delhi also did not oppose the convict's appeal in the High Court all that vehemently. Though its pleadings in the appeal are not available at the time of writing this, it is clear from the verdict that the Delhi Government did not strongly contest the High Court's verdict.

The Grounds of the Supreme Court

The Supreme Court of India found merit in the concurrent appeals before it preferred by the statutory National Commission for Women, led by a senior ruling party politician, belonging to the same political faction as the Delhi Government, and various left leaning women's organizations against the relief granted by the High Court.

The Supreme Court was responding to a vociferous campaign unleashed over press and visual media by the various organizations on the impropriety of the High Court's verdict. The High Court's verdict was termed retrograde and as setting a bad precedent. The primary ground for the attack from the NCW and women's groups was the grounds cited for the clemency.

If being able to join a prestigious service like the IAS is the criteria for leniency, they felt, that it would result in a differential treatment for educated and qualified accused and convicts. They felt that the education, qualifications or status of the accused/convict must not have a bearing on the punishment or sentence, much so with the length or gravity of the punishment. These judgments induce an elite bias, preference and easier defence in such heinous offences, they felt.

They also saw red in some recent different trial court attempts to factor the facts after the crime that the accused had married the victim as grounds to award suspended sentences. The extreme groups would argue that such sentences are extra legal and must not happen. Even if the accused has made good the victim's social stigma and given her a place of esteem, albeit after a period of sufferance, this act of 'compassion and redemption' must not be criteria in determining the quantum of sentence since it induced value biases in favour of the accused.

Besides since intimidation and threats for sexual favours or forced marriages are a very common Indian experience especially for rural based less educated women, such relief could further abet criminal elements that might resort to rape to secure consent as a first resort. So as a verdict involving huge safety and social ramifications, these judgments incentivize lawlessness and criminality in securing sexual access and dominating women, the groups felt. Agencies like police and panchayats may also take a cue from such signals and settle rape cases for considerations such as monetary compensation or marriage, further driving underreported crime still underground.

A very significant factor that went against ABC in the women's group's view was the fact that he qualified for the IAS, the premier service bestowed with both huge developmental and law and order responsibilities in both State and the Central governments. The presence of a rapist convict in the law enforcers role was viewed to be antithetical to the fundamental values of public life. Even if the government would appoint him he would find it near impossible to command respect or trust of the system. Some joked that he may be retained in Prison administration and could be made the Magistrate of all prisons of the country, and later Jails Secretary, etc.

Rape : More than a Criminal Problem

Rape is one of the crimes the Indian and South Asian criminal justice systems are finding hard to tackle. This is because of the patriarchal male domination in society and polity is partially permissive to the idea of subjugation of women sometimes even using violence on their corporal self as admissible socially. Some chosen data will supplement this point.

Rape has shown a 700 per cent jump from 1971 prevalence as per the Indian National official crime data. In 2008 first three quarters alone 18,000 incidents were officially registered. While murder (100%), kidnapping and abduction (149%) went up substantially in the period, dacoity came down by 16 per cent. Indian criminal records system started recording rape data only from 1971. The profiling of the rapists reveals that 73 per cent are committed by persons known to victims and 10 per cent were even relatives. A significant number of victims were minors. In India one rape related crime is reported every 18 minutes.

A comparison with an advanced industrial economy like USA is interesting. Though patriarchy has significantly subsided there and legal economic status gap between genders have converged, the offence of rape is very prevalent indeed. Surveys show that one-sixth of women in the reproductive age are at least one time victims of rape or attempted rape. College aged women are four times more likely to be raped. In 2007, there were 2,48,300 issues of sexual assault and one rape occur every two minutes. Surprisingly it is estimated that only 40 per cent of incidents are ever complained upon. US Government monitors the reporting rates and it is seen that reporting has increased by 30 per cent since 1993.

Recent developments like the Priyadarshini Mattoo case (India) and the Mukhtyar Mai case (Pakistan) have been significant policy change inducers beyond being test cases, were highly held patriarchal values have been challenged and criminality addressed by law courts in a firm manner. In the former case, Ms. Mattoo's rape-cum-murder resulted in a death sentence for the accused, one Mr. Santosh Singh. The victim, a 23 years old Law student from Delhi was attacked and brutally killed with multiple injuries, using a wire and motor cycle rider's helmet, after brutal rape by her stalking college mate. While the trial court set him free on the basis of lack of evidence based on local police and CBI investigation, the High Court of Delhi which found merit in the current accused's appeal had given death sentence to the accused. The High Court had spoken unequivocally on that occasion that "For a crime of this sort which has been committed with premeditation and in a brutal manner, the convict deserves only one sentence but death." Mr. Singh, the accused, was the son of a senior IPS officer. Interestingly the defence's pleas on the court giving a chance for rehabilitation in society were rejected equivocally by the Judges. The fact that the convict had since married and had a two years old girl child and family with sick elders to look after bore no weight with the Court's decision.

In another recent case of Rape of a German student in India, the accused was sentenced within record time, owing to rapid prosecution and faster court hearings. However, the accused, son of an influential police officer obtained parole and has gone absconding, making a mockery of legal process. Some IAS officers have been accused, arrested and tried of sexual misconduct, several officers face such charges.

The Mukhtyar Mai case has attracted global attention for the grave injustice committed on the lady belonging to Eastern Pakistan province where she was raped by the relatives of a higher tribe family's daughter on whom her brother seemed to have interest on. Interestingly the punishment to Ms. Mai was meted out as a revenge punishment by the tribal council (*Shura*) which allowed the petitioners—brother and father to rape her in revenge. In a sense it was local law legitimizing her violation. Her case upon appeal is in the regional High Court. Of late she decided to become the second wife of one of her police guards deputed to safeguard her.

The primaeval consideration that women's bodies are property to be enjoyed, sold or bartered, and the combat tactic of humiliating enemy at war time by raping their women, caste suppression, the use of *Prima Nocta* (Feudal first right to a newly wed) as a tactic of domination, and even widely held attitudes to violence by men are complicating factors in South Asia. For example 70 per cent of Indian women who responded to a national survey that there is nothing wrong if wives are occasionally beaten by husbands if she committed adultery or forgot to cook dinner. An equal consideration, therefore, is miles away if not light years.

Civil Services and Convicts

Membership and appointment to the IAS and other services in Government cannot be claimed as a matter of right with the government. Success in the UPSC examination does not guarantee a job or does not oblige Government of India to appoint anyone to any service. The fact that the subject has a criminal record can be held against him and appointment denied on such grounds. Even a conviction is not necessary for such denial, though such denial can be contested in courts under constitutional grounds.

However, in this case, while government has the discretion to grant such clemency, the High Court had jumped the gun and not bothered to hear the Union of India as to whether the government is even appointing him in the first place. In fact the relevant sections of the High Court's orders would reveal a presumption that he is going to secure appointment in view of his success in the examination. In other words, the High Court's verdict became a curtain raiser for the legal battle that Mr. ABC was to unleash on Government of India to get it to appoint him, as soon as he secured his release from prison. He stood good chances of making it to the prestigious portals of the IAS, the LBSNAA in Mussoorie where he would hope to blend with the other trainees, for whom he might be curiosity for a while, and turn a leaf in his very chequered career so far.

The Supreme Court stayed the release orders of the Delhi High Court and gave indications that the order was flawed. It has sought the opinion of the Government of India regarding his suitability and eligibility of the appointment and also Delhi Government to counter the appeal of the women's groups. In the mean time his fate hangs in balance and he is still incarcerated.

The Issues

1. While there may be merit in the High Court's findings on evidence in the case before the trial court, its reversal of the trial courts guilty finding citing the same set of evidences, as in the issue of consent, reveals the divergence in interpretation possible on the same set of facts. Did the trial court act in haste and harshly to Mr. ABC and was the High

Court genuinely trying to rectify what it was a miscarriage of justice?

2. Did the High Court however err on the grounds it took refuge to curtail the sentence of Mr. ABC and recommend his release? Did it not create an impression that an *Obiter* was being used to form precedent and substantial decisions being taken on presumption of good behaviour and abstract moral terms like redemption?
3. If the High Court was evidence-wise convinced that Mr. ABC was punished unfairly and without ground why did it not grant an acquittal and settled the matter? Do not elements of crime of abetting remain in the way the High Court refused him a clean chit?
4. Was the High Court's motive above suspicion? Especially in the light of the State playing a passive role in the appeal before High Court?
5. On the other hand, a position in a confusing, not "fully" proven crime of passion that the convict is fully beyond redemption and must never be integrated with the community and civil society also is very extreme and fundamentally conflicting with the objectives of justice. Retribution in the justice system is to deter and prevent, after the convict has undergone the prescribed and legally enforced punishment, he/she has to be fully rehabilitated and integrated into the mainstream society. The case of Mr. ABC would have been a true eye opener and a great hope for all young prisoners erred in the past but genuinely hope to redeem themselves and find productive roles in society after the punishment. Mr. ABC's appointment would have given a great demonstration to the correction capability of our prison administration and criminal justice system.
6. But the damage it would have done to the morale of thousands of victims and their families of sex abuse and rape must be a valid counter point. If the Union Government and higher judiciary help a rape convict get appointed as a district magistrate, the king pin of local administration of law and order in India, it could be argued that the system would suffer a loss of credibility and character. The senior services would

also suffer from breach of public trust and have negative media fallout. But while senior officers may fully oppose this, they fail to bring to book the numerous criminals and colluders who continue unabated or uninterrupted in the various services including IAS and IPS. What can a young entrant damage more than the damage inflicted by dozens of serving unpunished rapists who use their position of power and prestige to hide their crimes?

7. The selective engagement of the NCW and Women's groups is also politically charging the clear minded appreciation of the facts in the case. Is it fair on Mr. ABC to be made a victim of demonstrability, a reality circus while his case may have merit on the basis of evidence, if he were in fact selected for an inconsequential job like that of a bank clerk or in the private sector, would his case have been better served? Is he being discriminated since he sought membership in a most hated service of the country? Should criminal trials address political points? Are they venues of demonstrating to the national or community norms or venues of assessing guilt and culpability of the individual?

Task

Assume that Supreme Court of India has called for Government of India's view point and you are the Secretary Personnel of the Union of India and your Minister has sought a clear advice in the matter. Please draft a policy memo with clear recommendations to what stand Government of India must take in the matter before the Supreme Court of India. (Maximum words 500)?

4

Gas Trouble

A Case in LPG Distribution Services

Prasanth N.

Civil Supplies was one area of special interest to District Collector, Kozhikode, Kerala. He would say that this is one of those areas in which intervention as District Magistrate and Executive Magistrate is still necessary. He had on many occasions mentioned that the LPG dealers in the District were behaving like ruffians to the customers and the number of complaints had gone up immensely. Months back, he had handed me a complaint that had come to him from an LPG consumer regarding delivery charges. The issue was that the LPG dealers were demanding delivery charges beyond the permitted rates. That particular case was enquired and found that not much could be done on it. The dealer had with him orders to justify his action and I reported accordingly to the Collector.

However, the Collector urged me to go to the legal root of the issue and see if something could be done on this since a lot of complaints were coming up. During the Collector's conference in the State headquarters, the issue of irregularities committed by the LPG dealers had come up for discussion and the Government had directed all District Collectors to rein in the dealers. The issue of excess charging in the name of delivery charges was a major allegation. No bill was ever given for such payment. This was not only 'black marketing' but also evasion of tax and generating black money! The money thus illegally generated in the whole of Kozhikode District for a month amounted to 12 crores by conservative estimation.

So I set about "researching" LPG delivery/supply/transportation and the laws covering it.

So, the Act, orders and regulations concerning LPG supply were procured. *Liquefied Petroleum Gas (Regulation of Supply and Distribution) Order, 2000* made under Section 3 of the *Essential Commodities Act, 1955 (10 of 1955), Explosives Act* and *Kerala Petroleum Products Dealers Licencing Order, (KPPDL Order) 1981* formed the basic legal framework.

From the HPCL, BPCL and IOC websites, the dealer application forms were downloaded. These prescribed the requirements/pre-qualifications of a person to be eligible to be appointed as a dealer. The website further informed that an agreement would be executed with the dealer. In my capacity as an Executive Magistrate, I summoned the copies of the agreement between the Oil Companies and the dealers. I issued letters to the dealers in the city citing that a comprehensive effort was being undertaken to improve the LPG delivery mechanism. The dealers submitted the copies of the agreements. The revelations were interesting.

The dealer application forms revealed that the LPG distributors were selected and appointed by the Oil Companies on the basis of their competence and willingness to make free home delivery to the consumers, amongst other conditions. The commission for the dealers was to cover the cost of making the home deliveries also. The requirements specified for an applicant to secure an Indane-dealership, as mentioned in the application document Clause 8.3:

> "INFRASTRUCTURE FOR HOME DELIVERY OF LPG CYLINDERS: *In addition to showroom and godown for storage of filled LPG cylinders, delivery vehicles will be required for effecting **free home delivery** of Indane cylinders in their area of operation.*"

The same clause was found in the Dealership application of other Oil Companies also. The Dealership Agreement entered into between the Oil Company and the Gas Agency specifically mentions that the dealer has to make free home delivery to the customer. Dealership Agreement made with HPCL (Clause 5), Indane (Clause 4) and Bharat Gas (Clause 4) read:

> "The dealer **shall at his own cost and without charging any extra to the consumers** arrange for delivery of full cylinders from his own storage premises to the customers' premises and for the return of empty cylinders from the customers' premises to his own approved storage premises."

Now, I got excited about my discovery and drafted an Order to be issued by the Collector that would prohibit levy of delivery charges.

But then, the District Civil Supplies Officer (DSO) showed me a Circular issued by the Oil Companies specifying 'free-delivery zone' and allowing for the collection of charges for delivery beyond certain distances. Once this was brought to my notice I felt that there was no point in going any further. If it had been okayed by the Oil Company, what could the government do about it? After all, there is the principle of "privity of contract". I informed this to the Collector, who simply said, "There must be something…just keep looking".

And there was something! This had not struck me in the beginning.

Rule 9 of the Liquefied Petroleum Gas (Regulation of Supply and Distribution) Order, 2000 made in exercise of the powers conferred by Section 3 of the Essential Commodities Act, 1955 (10 of 1955) reads:

> "….(d) No distributor shall sell liquefied petroleum gas at a higher price than that fixed by the Government Oil Company or the parallel marketer.
>
> (e) No distributor shall, without prior written permission of the concerned Government Oil Company, refuse to make home delivery at the address of the consumer, as registered with the distributor.
>
> *Provided that the* State **Government** may, *fix additional charges for home delivery of LPG cylinders to the consumers, as it may deem necessary in view of the geographical terrain and/or the distance in the area of distribution."*

It meant that a Government order was required to allow and determine delivery charges. The Oil Company can only permit a distributor to refuse home delivery to a certain registered address of a customer. [Rule 9(e) of the *LPG Order, 2000*]. The Company has no authority to determine or demarcate 'free-delivery zone' or to fix any charges. Any additional charge for home delivery may be fixed by the Government alone, considering the geographical terrain and area of distribution. This provision was incorporated in view of difficult and mountainous terrains with far-flung settlements spanning large areas wherein economical operations are difficult and dealers are not forthcoming. In States like Assam, Meghalaya, Uttarakhand, Arunachal Pradesh and Sikkim this was necessary to attract competitive application from prospective dealers.

So, the circular limiting pre-delivery area issued by the Oil Companies unilaterally was found to be illegal, *ultra vires* and against the *Liquefied Petroleum Gas (Regulation of Supply and Distribution) Order, 2000* made under Section 3 of the *Essential Commodities Act, 1955* (10 of 1955). There was no Government Order sanctioning such a colleetion of money.

In Kozhikode District, dealers of major Oil Companies are evenly spread out and are operating in a competitive environment with no geographical or logistical hindrance. The agreed area of distribution is of a few kilometres only and there is no dearth of willing agents to take up distribution. Therefore, it was clear that there is no case for additional charges to be imposed on the consumers. Considering the above facts and the legal aspects involved, I drafted an Order for the Collector. The new order made LPG home-delivery free for customers. This was approved by the Collector, but not immediately publicised. The Collector suggested that I reveal this in the next LPG Adalat on 13/11/2008. This would naturally stir a hornet's nest, and to explain the position, he would hold a press briefing.

On 13/11/2008 I chaired the LPG Adalat for Koyilandy Taluk on behalf of the District Collector. Lots of complaints against the LPG dealers were taken up. In one particular case, there was a complaint regarding non-home delivery of cylinders. The allegation was that cylinders were left before a provision store from where people were supposed to collect it. Even as the Adalat was going on, I directed the Village Officer of the concerned place to check this particular location and see if cylinders were indeed stocked in that shop. He reported in the affirmative. I ordered Rs. 20,000 as fine then and there, after recording the dealer's Statement. (I also instructed the Village Officer to give the report in writing.) Many other cases were settled in the Adalat. There were a lot of queries and complaints regarding delivery charge and free delivery zone. Bulk of the complaints were regarding the overlooking of priority and charging of up to Rs. 100 for making delivery within small distances.

At the end of the Adalat, I presented before the audience, the new Order of the Collector that prohibited collection of delivery charges. I read out the Order, explained why it was being issued and how strictly it would be implemented. The moment I finished, there was a thunderous applause from the audience. Alongside there were protests and murmurs from the dealers! One of the dealers said (threatened) that there would be law and order problems if this 'one-sided' order was implemented. I assured him not to worry on that count, as the District Administration was capable of maintaining law and order.

I informed the Collector of this. Since the Order was now in public domain, the LPG dealers were gearing in for a strike. The Collector held a press briefing to explain this Order and the rationale behind it. The Channels gave screaming 'Flash news'. Generally, the reaction was extremely positive. But the LPG dealers had also started their game to upset our applecart.

On 18/11/2008, as directed by the Collector, 6 teams led by the RDO, 4 Deputy Collectors and myself were formed. We descended upon 6 LPG dealers within the city and conducted a detailed inspection/raid. Irregularities were numerous. There were violation of LPG Order 2000 and Gas Cylinder Rules, offences punishable under the Essential Commodities Act and Explosives Act. None of them possessed a licence under the Kerala Petroleum Product Licensing Order, 1981. (This was an issue, which was discussed in the Collector's Conference as well. It was directed that all Collectors should take steps to ensure that the dealers were encouraged into applying for the licence under KPPDL Order.) The reports were compiled and transferred to the police to charge criminal cases. These raids were widely reported in the media and it created the impression that the District Administration meant business.

The Order was popular with the public who were fed up with the greedy LPG dealers. But the LPG dealers apparently teamed up. My Confidential Assistant got information from an LPG dealer that money was being collected and political mobilisation was on by the dealers.

The Collector was duly asked the order to withdraw. The Collector explained the legal position and expressed his helplessness. The

Secretary to Government (Civil Supplies) issued a letter *reinstating status quo*. However, since this was not a Government Order, it had no legal sanctity and could not be followed since it violated the Act and the orders made thereunder. The story was taking a spicy turn. . . .

Confronted with the issue, the Minister for Civil Supplies called for a meeting in Trivandrum. I reached Trivandrum and called on the Civil Supplies Director and briefed her on the issue. When I explained the facts, she said that it would be nice if I represented the version of the District Administration before the Minister. As of now, it was a one sided affair with the LPG dealers presenting a very biased view. I called up my Collector and with his permission attended the meeting on behalf of the District administration.

By evening I went with the Director to the Minister's office. The Minister for Civil Supplies chaired the meeting held in his chamber. The Secretary, Civil Supplies Commissioner, Civil Supplies Director, representatives of the LPG Dealers Association and myself attended the meeting.

The meeting started with the dealers attacking the Collector. They tried to play the Secretary to Government. against the Collector. They made wild allegations hinting that the Collector had dismissed the Secretary's letter with contempt. The raids on the LPG dealers were also given another colour, that of personal animosity and what not ! The representatives of the LPG Dealers were Trivandrum based and obviously did not know me. Once I got introduced the vitriolic tongues cooled down; basically because now they knew that what they spoke will reach the Collector's ears. Second, they could not bluff. I could personally vouch for the proper conduct of the raid. I put forth our arguments.

I did what I was assigned to do. I argued to the best of my ability. I brought in the issue of Kerala Petroleum Products Dealers Licensing Order, (KPPDL Order) 1981. None of the LPG dealers had taken licence under this Order. It was an Order made under Essential Commodities Act and had stringent provisions. The meeting ended with a pro-dealer decision, possibly to avert a confrontation. The Minister asked for a commitment that *status quo* would be restored. Then I said that I am just an IAS Trainee who was not competent to give any assurance or commitment. The Minister laughed and said, "yes, yes," and then proceeded to summarise his decision. I realized that even honest and upright politicians tend to get misled by circumstances. The Secretary, as directed by the Minister, issued a Government letter to the District Collector in this regard.

The media carried this news with prominence. I felt bad. We had law and good intent on our side, yet we lost. We were helpless before powers that were. Besides, my loyalty to my boss made me feel doubly bad. The orders were issued based on my legal call and confidence that it would be upheld in any forum.

My Collector, however, had a trump up his sleeve. He acknowledged Minister's order. He asked me to draft another Order with an innocuous looking rider...***the delivery charges would stand restored to all LPG dealers who have a licence to operate.*** Now, none of these LPG dealers had a licence under KPPDL Order ! Nobody could say that the dealers need not obtain licences. . . .

The dealers were mighty frustrated with this. They had got nothing ! So a State-wide strike on 26/11/2008 was called. They publicly vowed to transfer out the District Collector. A meeting was called by the Government on 25/11/2008 to avert the strike. Again I went to Trivandrum, to represent the Collector. This meeting was chaired by the Secretary, who gave a soothing talk to the dealers; but yielded nothing. The dealers were clearly told that they would have to apply for licence under KPPDL Order. There was no provision to put a Government Order in abeyance. So the strike was on.

The strike was a tactical blunder on the part of the dealers. Now this Kozhikode-specific issue got attention all over the State. Despite the strike, the dealers did not stop the supply to highly valued customers like Star hotels and restaurants. This discrimination against the common man was highlighted by the media. We continued to enforce the LPG Order, both in letter and spirit. The public support was obvious and the huge number of complainants who came forward bore testimony to the faith in the District Administration. The Collector took special care that there was timely intervention in the complaints and I was put in charge of co-ordinating the same.

The LPG dealers' association meanwhile went to the High Court challenging the Order of the Collector. The High Court not only upheld the Collector's Order but commented that such upright officers are necessary for the society! Now transferring out the Collector became a remote possibility as it would be seen negatively by the public. So he stayed on. LPG Order and related laws were enforced with increased zeal.

Post Script: Having failed to annul the Collector's order, the LPG dealers challenged the Sanctity of KPPDL Order of 1981, and they got an order from the High Court quashing it. This was surprising, as the rationale cited would leave all State legislations on concurrent subjects null and void! Thus, the last straw on which we were holding on came through. It was obvious that the Government pleader did not exert himself the Government did not go in appeal.

My Collector was transferred out on 2/2/2009. A Government Order allowing for collection of delivery charges also came out.

We won many battles in this series but lost the war. . . . or maybe the battle is on and the war is far from over. Some consumer activists might take it up in the High Court and get it all reversed. . . . so hopes the optimist in me.

5

Police Firing in Nasarathpur

Sanjeev Chopra

Objective

The preventive magisterial jurisdiction provided for in chapter eight of the Cr.P.C. constitutes a powerful adjunct to executive authority. The case study aims to illustrate how the preventive sections of the Cr.P.C., particularly Sections 107 to 114 and prohibitory provisions of Section 144 of Cr.P.C. can be used to prevent crime and disturbance of public tranquillity and breach of peace. The case study also illustrates the application of Section 129 of the Cr.P.C., dealing with dispersal of unlawful assembly and Section 174 Cr.P.C. which deals with inquest by an Executive Magistrate.

Learning Points

The following learning points need to be highlighted:

1. An inquest needs to be conducted immediately after death is reported. This should preferably be done in the presence of the local public so that there is no room for any rumour or misinformation.
2. To reach the incident site on time is half the battle won. Response time of the district administration in the instant case was not satisfactory. It took more than an hour for a senior person to reach the spot located at a distance of barely one kilometre from the Collectorate/District Police Office. In fact, although DSP was directed by the SP to rush to the spot at 12 noon, he reached only around 1 PM along with

the ADM. It is also disconcerting to note that the officer in charge of the local PS was not kept in the loop to begin with. This also raises a question about the communication system and the use of mobile phones. SP was directly contacted by the local public and he too, instead of instructing the OIC, asked the DSP to rush to the spot. OIC is the first line of defence and many a time better equipped, due to his knowledge of the area and local people, to control the situation. It is also a failure of the ADM that he could not bring down the tempers. This was not a major problem to begin with and the ADM should have been able to control it by displaying a neutral persona without siding with the JMFC. The incident also has lessons about the way mobile courts should be conducted. Prior intimation needs to be given to the SP so that adequate arrangements can be made to maintain the authority of the court. Megaphone must be carried in vehicle by public officials involved in law and order duties.

3. At the end of the first day, on which the firing took place, the DM and SP may jointly chalk out a strategy to control the situation. This strategy may, *inter alia*, comprise the following:

   (a) Sanction some *ex gratia* amount from the Red Cross to those killed in the police firing. Also move the State Government to provide rehabilitation assistance to the affected families.
   (b) Mobilise additional police force by contacting the police headquarters.
   (c) Provide security to places which are the likely target of public anger.
   (d) Divide the town into sectors and introduce intensive patrolling.
   (e) Flag March may be ordered, if required. The flag march is a message for the people that the police is the guardian of peace and keen to provide the citizens safety of their lives and property.
   (f) Police pickets may be put up at crucial locations.
   (g) Intelligence machinery may be activated to seek

information about the public mood and agitation proposed, if any.

(h) FIRs to be immediately filed against those who could be identified as part of the unlawful assembly which indulged in rioting.

(i) Use the preventive sections of the Cr.P.C. to round up the anti-socials.

(j) Extend prohibitory orders under Section 144 Cr.P.C. till such time the situation warrants. The enforcement of the orders also needs to be ensured. While the orders are in force, a crowd of 1,000 persons gathered at Central Market in the morning of October 13. Instead of dispersing the crowd, the Collector sought the advice of some eminent citizens residing near the market!

(k) To build public opinion against the hooligans, immediately open lines of communication to eminent citizens of the locality including public representatives.

(l) Issue daily press releases to keep the public posted about all developments, action taken and stem the flow of rumours. Press Conference may be conducted on the second day to brief the media on the incident, announce *ex gratia* for the deceased/injured and also announce the names of the constable(s) suspended.

4. Form a Peace Committee and organize regular meetings. The Peace Committee may have representatives from all walks of society, including the public representatives. As one of the persons killed was a student, some student leaders may also be taken as members, in the Peace Committee. Once the situation begins to normalize, a Peace March may be organised. Wide publicity may be given to the proposed march and all sections of the society may be requested to participate. Peace March, if timed correctly and organised with wide participation, normally gives good results; tempers come down, mood lightens and a signal goes out that things are returning to normal.

5. One should not give way in operational matters to seniors, who reach the site, unless one is convinced of the suggestion being made. Ultimate responsibility rests with the DM and

SP in law and order matters. The advice of seniors may be sought for, if required, but the final decision is that of the DM and SP.

6. Although it did not lead to an untoward situation, sending back the force from the Collectorate on the second day may not be considered as a wise step. The mob mentality cannot be overcome by reason or logic. Sending back the police force emboldened the mob to make wild allegations against the government officials and the Collector himself. There was a strong possibility that the Collector and SDM could have been taken hostage demanding the handing over of the erring police personnel. The situation could have taken a very ugly turn putting the life of Collector and other officials at danger. The police force could have been asked to wait outside the main gate of the Collectorate rather than being sent back.

1. Introduction

Nasarathpur is a small, sleepy district headquarters town with a population of 80,000 persons approximately. It is famous all over the country for a twelfth century Shiva temple. As the legend goes, several hundred years ago, Lord Shiva appeared in a dream of the local king and told him that he had chosen his kingdom as his abode. He also mentioned that the presence of a bull (symbolizing *Nandi*, the carrier of Lord Shiva) on one of the innumerable hills dotting the kingdom would indicate the exact spot. On the morning of the next day, the king dispatched his soldiers in all directions and one of them spotted a bull grazing on a hill slope. The king ordered the construction of a Shiva temple on that hill top.

The town comes alive during the festival of *Shivaratri* when almost 1,00,000 pilgrims congregate from all over the country. The people of Nasarathpur are generally peace loving and the town has no history of any major law and order problem. Hence, when two people died in police firing on two consecutive days in October 2004, this surprised everybody. There was also a great deal of public resentment and uproar in the State Legislative Assembly over the occurrence. The Opposition in the State Assembly vehemently criticised the district administration especially for its failure to prevent the second day's firing and staged a walkout demanding a judicial inquiry into the incident. The Chief Minister, who was running a coalition government, was under pressure from his allies to take some "decisive" action to prove that it is a people's government.

2. Chronological Account

The following is a chronological account of the events as they took place during those three days in October 2004.

12.10.2004

10.30 A.M.

A mobile court starts functioning in the Central Market of Nasarathpur with Shri S. Kumar, J.M.F.C. as the Presiding Officer. The Assistant Controller, Weights and Measures and Health Officer of the Nasarathpur Municipality are also present. Shri S. Kumar, J.M.F.C., is holding a mobile court for the first time in his 3 years service career. The court mainly seeks to punish the offenders for petty offences under the Weights and Measures Act and for food adulteration. No earlier intimation about the holding of Mobile Court was given to either the Collector or the S.P. No Officer from the local police station was present. Only one court sub-inspector along with one constable accompanied the judicial party.

11.30 A.M.

Resentment brews with regard to the "excessive" quantum of fine. 13 cases are compounded in the court under the Weights and Measures Act and the I.P.C. The maximum amount of fine imposed was Rs. 1,000 under Weight and Measures Act. The Weight and Measures Act provides for a maximum fine of Rs. 5000 and the I.P.C. provides for a maximum fine of Rs. 1,000 under Sections 272 and 273.

12.00 Noon

Heated arguments take place between the J.M.F.C. and the prosecuting government servants on the one side and the traders on the other. The

S.P., who is conducting constables' recruitment examination in the Reserve Lines, is informed over his cell phone by a local citizen. He orders the DSP (Crime) to rush to the spot along with 2 sections of APR force.

12.30. P.M.

Situation worsens. People in the crowd and those on the roof tops start pelting stones on the government servants and vehicles. J.M.F.C. is injured and some vehicles damaged; strength of the crowd is approximately, 1,500.

12.45 P.M.

A.D.M. is informed as District Magistrate and Sub-Divisional Magistrate are away on a joint tour of Samardha, an interior Block of the district.

1.00 P.M.

A.D.M. reaches the spot along with the D.S.P. (Crime). He finds a crowd of more than 1,500, mostly traders, heckling the J.M.F.C. to stop the Mobile Court and refund the fine realised. A.D.M. appeals to the traders to disperse peacefully; advises them to abide by the law and respect the authority of the judiciary. This brings forth no response. Efforts are made by the A.D.M. to locate a megaphone/loudspeaker over which he can address the crowd so as to be audible but none is available. In the meantime, the A.D.M. is hit on the shoulder by a brick thrown from the roof top. A section of the crowd damages the approaching vehicles of the police and the fire brigade and injures the fire brigade staff. The A.D.M. is man-handled by the police constables demanding an order for firing.

1.20 P.M.

A police reinforcement party proceeding to the trouble spot is heavily brick batted and the windscreen of the van is broken. The driver of the van momentarily loses control of the vehicle and barely avoids running over some of the onlookers. A constable, who happens to be president of the District Constable Association, gets down from the police van and fires 3 rounds indiscriminately at a section of the violent crowd in which one person dies and another is injured. After the firing, the police van reverses and immediately leaves for the reserve lines. The deceased is later identified as one Purusottam Sethi, brother of the President, Youth Wing of the Jana Morcha. The Jana Morcha is the ruling party in the State.

Meanwhile at the trouble spot, the violent assembly is declared unlawful by the A.D.M. and lathi charge and subsequently tear gassing is ordered to disperse the crowd.

1.30 P.M.

The S.P. reaches the spot along with one platoon of Armed Police and the violent crowd is chased away by severe lathi charge and the situation controlled. Due to the pelting of stones, 2 fire brigade vehicles, 3 police vehicles and one jeep of the Municipality are damaged. 16 police personnel, 5 fire brigade staff and 10 persons of Health and Weights and Measures Departments are injured, apart from the J.M.F.C.

3.00 P.M.

Prohibitory orders under Section 144 Cr.P.C. promulgated in the municipality area till 6 P.M. of 13.10.94. The President, Traders' Association consults the other office bearers of the Association and calls for Nasarathpur "Bandh" on 13.10.2004.

6.00 P.M.

After receiving information about the firing, the District Magistrate and the Sub-Divisional Magistrate return to headquarters. The D.I.G. of police, who is stationed in the nearby district, also reaches around the same time.

9.00 P.M.

The deceased is carried away from the District Headquarters Hospital by friends and relatives in a peaceful procession and cremated.

9.30 P.M.

District Magistrate and Sub-Divisional Magistrate visit the house of the deceased to offer their condolences. The DIG of police, briefs the Finance Minister, the most powerful among the Cabinet Ministers and number two in the pecking order, who enjoys full confidence of the Chief Minister about the incidents at Nasarathpur. The DIG is asked by the Finance Minister to keep the police visibility to the minimum as a great deal of resentment exists against the police. He is also instructed to ensure that no further untoward situation develops, as it would adversely affect the chances of the ruling party in the ensuing bye-elections to the Nasarathpur Parliamentary Constituency, necessitated due to sudden demise of the sitting MP in a road accident. DIG passes on these instructions to SP for compliance.

13-10-2004

1.00 A.M.

Four local MLAs arrive at Nasarathpur Circuit House from the State Capital where the Assembly is in session. No prior intimation about their arrival is given to the district administration. In the meantime, around midnight, the erring police constable responsible for the unauthorized firing is identified and suspended by S.P.

6.30 A.M.

Some young traders along with some anti-social elements start congregating near Central Market. They seek to mobilise the student community in view of the fact that the deceased was a student of the local college. After some time they start shouting slogans and putting up road blockades.

8.30 A.M.

The Sub-Divisional Magistrate goes to the Town Police Station to ascertain the situation in the town in the aftermath of the yesterday's firing. He is informed by the Inspector-in-Charge that the situation is normal and no untoward incident has been reported from any part of the Town. However, when he proceeds to the Central Market, he finds a highly agitated crowd of about 1000 persons gathered near the place of firing shouting anti-police slogans. The District Magistrate is informed of the development. The District Magistrate consults some eminent citizens of the town staying near the Central Market, who opine that coercive measures may be counter productive and the crowd would gradually disperse after shouting slogans. The President, Traders' Association calls for a general body meeting at 11 AM which is to be attended by the local MLAs.

11.15 A.M.

In course of the meeting of Traders Association, the local MLAs, all belonging to the ruling party, are severely heckled about their inability to provide any benefit/protection to the trading community. The traders present recount the harassment they routinely face at the hands of government functionaries. Some of the traders allege the involvement of the local MLAs in the corrupt practices and question them as to why some of the government officers, known to be harassing the traders, have not been transferred, in spite of their repeated requests. The discussion gradually heats up and the MLAs are man-handled and roughed up by the younger traders. The President, Traders Association tries in vain to bring a semblance of order in the meeting. To somehow escape from the imbroglio, the MLAs offer to take up the grievances of traders with the Collector.

11.30 A.M.

A highly unruly mob is "led" to the Collectorate by the local MLAs. However, the crowd is not in control of the MLAs who are themselves being heckled and seeking protection in the Collectorate. As the gates of the Collectorate are locked, everyone jumps the boundary wall to enter the Collectorate.

11.45 A.M.

The District Magistrate and the SDM, monitoring the situation from the Residential Office of DM, rush to the Collectorate, upon being informed about the mob's entry. The vehicle carrying one platoon of Armed Police stationed in the Collectorate for its protection is gheraoed by the mob who are shouting anti-police slogans. Both the front and the rear doors of the Collectorate are locked and hardly any open space is available. The District Magistrate instructs the police force to withdraw and report at the Town Police Station. The police platoon sent back by the Collector reaches the Town Police Station in a highly agitated State for having been turned away by the District Magistrate. In the meantime, the MLAs quietly slip away from the Collectorate.

11.55 A.M.

The DM makes repeated appeals to pacify the crowd. A section of the crowd shouts slogans to the effect that all government servants, including the DM, are thieves and parasites. The crowd demands to hand them over the erring police personnel, an immediate order for judicial inquiry and dismissal of the enforcement staff of the Weights and Measures Department and Nasarathpur Municipality. The District Magistrate takes a calculated risk by telling the crowd, that the process of identification is going on and the constables responsible would be identified soon. Collector requests time till 4 PM for identification and the crowd agrees to disperse peacefully. At this point of time the DM and SDM were negotiating with a crowd of 1,000 approximately, the police force having been sent back.

1.15 P.M.

While dispersing from the Collectorate, a section of the crowd attacks and inflicts minor damage to the nearby Municipality Office. Stones are also pelted at the residence of the S.P., D.M. and S.D.M. intervene and persuade them to withdraw. In the State Assembly, uproarious scenes are witnessed and the entire opposition stages a walkout demanding a judicial inquiry. The Chief Minister orders for an inquiry by the Revenue Divisional Commissioner.

1.30 P.M.

While negotiations are going on at the Collectorate, a group of miscreants reach the Town Police Station and start pelting stones. Gradually, the crowd swells to an extremely violent mob of about 2,000. There follows a strong attack on the police station which is having 4 platoons of armed police. The Executive Magistrate orders for tear gas and lathi charge which prove to be in effective. Upon this, one round of fire is ordered which does not yield much result and a section of the crowd attempts to set afire the police van parked outside the Police Station. Around the same time, the Home Secretary speaks to the D.M. over telephone to ascertain the situation and advises him to avoid any further firing.

1.45 P.M.

Upon hearing of the development at the Town PS, the D.M., present in the Residence Office of S.P., wants to proceed to the spot along with some police force. However, it is discovered that the police force has been sent for lunch to the Reserve Lines by the DIG. When the DM remonstrates with the S.P., he remarks "*Why are you telling me all this? I am just a probationer out here*."

1.55 P.M.

In the meantime another round of fire is ordered at the Town PS in which one casualty takes place. This makes the crowd disperse and the situation is controlled.

In course of the day, sporadic incidents of arson take place and the miscreants put up road blocks all over the town. The offices of the Addl. District Medical Officer (Public Health) and Asstt. Controller (Weights and Measures) and the residence of the Municipality doctor are ransacked and damaged. Two clerks and one peon in office of the Weights and Measures are also injured in the attack.

6.00 P.M.

Prohibitory orders under Section 144 Cr.P.C. are extended for 3 more days. The President, Traders Association calls an emergency meeting of the executive council and decides to observe "bandh" on 14th and

15th October also. The DM opens dialogue with the traders and eminent citizens to restore normalcy.

9.00 P.M.

I.G. (Law and Order) arrives from the State Police Headquarters and reviews the situation.

14.10.2004

11.00 A.M.

Office bearers of the Traders Association led by its President and some eminent citizens meet the DM and submit a charter of 4 demands including that of a judicial inquiry and suspension of Asstt. Controller (Weights and Measures) and the Health Officer of the Municipality.

2.30 P.M.

News is flashed in the local TV channel regarding death of a beggar near the Town Police Station due to assault by the poiice men in course of patrolling. Rattled and sweating profusely, Collector and SP rush to the spot.

3. Dramatis Personae

Collector and DM

The DM has been working in Nasarathpur for the past one and a half years and enjoys a good reputation and public contact. This is his first stint as DM. He has toured the interior areas extensively and the district has done extremely well in rural development and poverty alleviation programmes under his stewardship. He maintains a good rapport with the District Judge and interacts with him socially, as well.

Superintendent of Police

The S.P. is a very gentle person who has joined the service about six years back. He was on leave for about one year after finishing probation, exploring other career options. His wife is a doctor from Rohsang who is feeling professionally frustrated in Nasarathpur. The S.P. belongs to the national capital and is bidding time till his Central deputation, for which he has been trying for the past one year, comes through. It is important for him to obtain an excellent annual appraisal to facilitate his central deputation.

Deputy Inspector General of Police

The D.I.G. is having an extremely dubious reputation and is known to be a puppet in the hands of the ruling party. He has a habit of dealing with the Officers-in-Charge of the Police Stations directly bypassing the S.P. On many occasions, he has transferred the Officers-in-Charge of police stations without the knowledge of S.P. who only received a copy of the order. Intra-district transfers of OICs are carried out by the S.P. as per rules. Once on any district tour, he completely takes over, making the S.P. redundant.

President, Nasarathpur Traders' Association

The President, Nasarathpur Traders' Association is also the Vice President of district unit of the People's Forum, the main opposition party. His firm is the local dealer of reputed national companies manufacturing pump sets and other agricultural equipments. The Zilla Parishad, of which Collector is the Chief Executive Officer, is the major customer of his firm which is procuring these equipments for supply to BPL families under the anti-poverty programmes. He meets the Collector quite regularly where he begins the discussion by taking up issues on behalf of the opposition and towards the end also slips in his personal business matters especially the question of delayed payments by the ZP to his firm.

Assistant Controller, Weights and Measures

The Assistant Controller has put in about 30 years of service and belongs to the neighbouring district. He was suspended last year for conniving with the petrol pump owners in tampering with the meter. After 14 months under suspension, he was reinstated 3 months back with the intervention of the local MLA who also helped him to secure a posting in the district. The Assistant Controller had reportedly visited the Central Market of Nasrathpur a couple of days back to extort money from the traders.

ANNEXURE-I

Relevant Statutory Provisions for conducting Mobile Court

1. The Provisions of Cr.P.C. under which Mobile Courts are Constituted

Courts of Judicial Magistrates (Section 11 Cr.P.C.)

In every district (not being a metropolitan area), there shall be established as many Courts of Judicial Magistrates of the first class and of the second class and at such places, as the State Government may, after consultation with the High Court, by notification, specify.

The Presiding officers of such Courts shall be appointed by the High Court.

2. Definition of Petty Offences

"Petty Offence" means any offence punishable only with fine not exceeding ***rupees one thousand***, but does not include any offence so punishable under the Motor Vehicles Act, 1939, or under any other law which provides for convicting the accused person in his absence on a plea of guilty. [S. 206(2)]

The State Government may, by notification, specially empower any Magistrate to exercise the powers conferred by sub-section (1) in relation to any offence which is compoundable under Section 320 or any offence punishable with ***imprisonment for a term not exceeding three months***, or with fine, or with both where the Magistrate is of opinion that, having regard to the facts and circumstances of the case, the imposition of fine only would meet the ends of justice. [S. 206(3)]

3. The Offences under the Weights and Measures Act and IPC which are 'Petty Offences'

The Standards of Weights and Measures Act, 1976

Section	*Offence*	*Penalty*
58	Penalty for contravention of S.35 (i.e., Manufactures, sellers, distributors, etc., to maintain records and registers)	Fine which may extend one thousand rupees (for first offence)
64	Penalty for contravention of S. 47 (i.e., persons exporting or importing any weight measure to get themselves registered)	Fine which may extend one thousand rupees (for first offence)

The Standards of Weights and Measures (Enforcement) Act, 1985

Section	*Offence*	*Penalty*
38(1)	Penalty for sale or delivery of commodities, etc., by non-standard weight or measure	Fine which shall not be less than rupees five hundred but which may extend to rupees two thousand (for first offence)
38(2)	Penalty for rendering service in terms of any weight, measure or number other than the standard weight or measure	Fine which shall not be less than rupees five hundred but which may extend to rupees two thousand (for first offence)
45	Penalty for contravention of Section 22 (i.e., Prohibition of sale or use of unstamped weights or measures)	Fine which may extend to rupees one thousand
46	Penalty for contravention of Section 23 (i.e., manufacturer, dealer or repairer to maintain records and registers)	Fine which may extend to rupees one thousand (for first offence)
47	Penalty for contravention of Section 24 (i.e., Verification and stamping of weights and measures)	Fine which may extend to rupees five hundred (for first offence)
48	Penalty for contravention of Section 28 (i.e., Power of Inspector to require Production of weights or measures or records for inspection)	Fine which may extend to rupees one thousand (for first offence)
52	Penalty for contravention of Section 35 (i.e., Sale by heaps)	Fine which may extend to rupees one thousand (for first offence)

Indian Penal Code

Section	*Offences*	*Penalty*
272	Adulteration of food or drink intended for sale	Six months imprisonment or with fine which may extend to rupees one thousand or with both
273	Sale of noxious food or drink	Six months imprisonment or with fine which may extend to rupees one thousand or with both

4. Section 4 of Police Act, 1861 provides that—The administration of the police throughout a general police district shall be vested in an officer to be styled the Inspector General of Police, and in such Deputy Inspectors General and Assistant Inspectors General as to the State Government shall deem fit.

The administration of the police throughout the local jurisdiction of the Magistrate of the district shall, under the general control and direction of such Magistrate, be vested in a District Superintendent and such Assistant District Superintendents, as the State Government shall consider necessary.

6

Tackling Commercial Encroachment

Prasanth N.

I joined as Assistant Collector (under trainee) at Kozhikode on the forenoon of 16th June, 2008. The Collector asked me one question on day one: "Do you want to work or do you want to freak out? This year is the last chance to freak out! ...." I said I wanted to work.

The Collector gently opened his table and took out a list and read it out. It contained the works he had identified for me. Soon, I was handed many files that involved some legal aspect or the other considering my law background. This innocent bunch of files included those regarding Best India Steel be and all the knotty legal issues associated with it.

In the next two or three days, I somehow managed to finish studying the voluminous files concerning the Best India Steel Co. issue.

Best India Steel Co. was established in 1963-64 on land acquired by the Government and given to the Company at a cheap rate. This land is now prime property. The Company shut down in the nineties and the majority stake in the Company was taken by industrialist and businessman Mr. Vivek Menon, who had many business interests in the Gulf countries. He also happens to be a member of Rajya Sabha. He also owned Jhelum Motors Ltd. (chain of motor vehicle showrooms). He had set up his car showroom and hi-tech workshop/ garage in the company land and was making money while the workers were conveniently laid off. Land of 4.18 acres was thus transferred illegally to Jhelum Motors Co. Ltd. (This was against the Land Acquisition Act provisions) and this had developed into a political tussle as well. The Company meanwhile was not paying up Rs. 68 lakhs to the Government as sales tax and other liabilities. Revenue recovery proceedings were conducted and a piece of land was attached, which, however, continued to be occupied by the Company.

The Collector wanted me to chart out a path for handling this case; proceeding along all three routes, i.e. eviction of encroachment, revenue recovery of pending Rs. 68 lakhs and action on violation of agreement when land was acquired for the Company. I was given full independence to chart out the path and the Tahsildar was given directions by the Collector to follow my directions in the matter.

Surprisingly, the Collectorate files did not have any details about the Company. We did not even know who the authorized signatory of the Company was. The communications with the Company, including notices, were being made on the address of Jhelum Motors Ltd., assuming that both were owned by the same person, Shri Vivek Menon, MP. This would prove to be a costly legal mistake.

The issue basically involved three Acts and three routes to be followed simultaneously.

- Land Acquisition Act;
- Revenue Recovery Act; and
- Kerala Land Conservancy Act.

Eviction of Encroachment

After studying the entire set of files, I felt that Kerala Land Conservancy Act procedure to evict the encroachment would be the easiest fruit to pluck. RR and LA could be cumbersome. Just before leaving for Trivandrum, for an assignment there I led a party to conduct a survey on the land in issue and detected 32 cents of encroachment. (The media went hyper on the revenue survey being done on Shri Vivek Menon property! As directed by the Collector, I kept mum.) Notice under Form B of KLC Act was issued the very same day.

Something that was done differently here under the Kerala Land Conservancy Act, was the issuance of Form B Notice. I was told by the clerks and the Tahsildar that usually they issued Form 'CC' and made summary eviction. This was the procedure adopted in Munnar as well. They told me that the normal procedure which involved an opportunity for hearing was lengthy and tiresome. But I felt that this would be in violation of Natural Justice and would not stand the scrutiny of law. May be this was one reason why the Government was losing all cases in Munnar. Besides, I did not find any speed in the Form 'CC' route. The matter was pending for over 2 years. it really did not matter if we went for the Form B and Form C route afresh. It would not last 2 years in any case, I was very sure. I put forth this argument before the Collector and at once he agreed, I asked the Tehsildar to issue Notice in Form B, which is basically a show cause notice. Eviction would follow only after hearing was conducted. This would satisfy the Judiciary regarding the Natural Justice aspect.) Secondly, the notice was to be issued to Jhelum Motors Pvt. Ltd. and not to Best India Steel Co. as was being done before. This was because of the simple fact that the encroacher is Jhelum Motors Ltd. The Best India Co. may or may not have permitted/ facilitated such an occupation; but as far as encroachment is concerned, Best India Co. is a stranger. The fact that the owners are the same is irrelevant. Legally, the Company is a separate legal person and Jhelum Motors is a separate legal person.

The Jhelum Motors Ltd. replied that they were not encroachers and were operating in the said land with permission from Best India Steel Co. based on an agreement entered between them on 16 January, 2006. However, they did not produce the agreement.

The Kozhikode Tehsildar conducted a hearing on the show cause notice. After that a legally watertight reasoned Order was drafted and handed to the Tahsildar who issued it and issued Form C notice. It read:

> *"Notice under Section 12 of Kerala Land Conservancy Act, 1957 was issued on 21.6.2008 to M/s. Jhelum Motors Ltd. upon preliminary finding of encroachment of 32 cents of land on Government Bought-in-land of 1 acre in R.S. 17/1A upon survey conducted on 21/6/2008. The notice sought to show cause before 30/6/2008 why proceedings should not be taken and orders passed under the provisions of the said Act. M/s. Jhelum Motors Ltd. filed a reply on 30.6.2008 claiming that their occupation was based on the licence procured from M/s. Best India Steel Co. Ltd dated 16.1.2006 covering 4.18 acres of land. The reply was without any material evidence to support their contention that the occupation of the land*

specified in the notice is legal. It was sought to implead M/s. Best India Steel Co. Ltd. as a party. An opportunity for hearing was sought which was immediately granted and posted for the next day, 1.7.2008 at 3.00 pm. Notices were issued accordingly, seeking M/s. Jhelum Motors Ltd. to produce all documents and evidence to support their claim and to present their case in detail during the hearing. It was decided not to issue any notice to Best India Steel Co. Ltd. as they are legally in no position to lease out Government land and are a total stranger in this particular case of land encroachment. It was up to the alleged encroacher to adduce evidence to support their claim to rightful possession of the land.

"On 1.7.2008 at 3.00 pm during the personal hearing granted, M/s. Jhelum Motors Ltd. filed a written Statement *admitting that they had no legal document to support their occupation of the aforementioned 32 cents. Neither could they produce a copy of the Licence Agreement claimed to be entered into with Best India Steel Co., to support their claim that they had occupied the said land* bona fide *believing that the latter held a good title over the same. The* Statement *claimed that the 32 cents in question had been vacated and handed over to M/s. Best India Steel Co. Ltd. at 10.30 am on the day of the hearing, 1.7.2008.*

"The survey conducted on 21.6.2008 had clearly shown an encroachment of 32 cents by M/s. Jhelum Motors Ltd. of the 1 acre of bought-in-land taken as such from M/s. Best India Steel Co. Ltd in 2004 notified and confirmed as well on 27.12.04. The Licence Agreement claimed to be entered into with Best India Steel Co. dated 16.1.2006 could in no way confer any right or claim to the land, which is government property. Any such claims are dilatory in purpose and without any legal acumen. Even after 11 days, M/s. Jhelum Motors Ltd. has failed to produce a single document supporting the legality of their occupation.

The 32 cents in question being allegedly vacated and handed over to M/s. Best India Steel Co. Ltd. at 10.30 am on the day of the hearing, despite being fully convinced that the

> *said property is government land and M/s. Jhelum Motors Ltd. trespassers themselves, having no authority to transfer such possession is illegal and* mala fide. *This is seen as a dilatory effort. The actual verification and survey conducted on 21.6.2008 had clearly shown an encroachment of 32 cents by M/s. Jhelum Motors Ltd. and establishment of a building and other assets on the same.*
>
> *"As such, it is deemed necessary to issue an Order accompanied by Notice under Form C to M/s. Jhelum Motors Ltd. seeking to vacate the unauthorized occupation failing which summary eviction will be resorted to.*
>
> *Dated 2nd July 1, 2008* *s/d*
> *Tahsildar, Kozhikode"*
>
> *When I reached back in Kozhikode, we went and took possession of the encroached land on 7.7.2008 for which Notice was issued under Form C. The office of M/s Jhelum Motors that was operating from 4.18 acres within this land was sealed and the land was taken back into possession of the Government.*

Now, I was fully convinced of my argument that 'Form B and Form C route' which involved formal hearing was better than summary eviction under Form 'CC'. The matter which was pending for 2 years despite using the 'summary' route could be settled in 2 weeks flat without resorting to any short-cut. The Collector told me that it was for the first time that they had not even gone for a petition in the High Court or procured a stay during the process. I was very happy that I could complete the first task that was entrusted by the Collector.

The directions given by the Collector during the whole process was excellent and reassuring. There was practically so much freedom to go about the whole thing that the feeling was very 'unreal'. It was a major issue in media. It was also during this process that I had my first interaction with the media in my official capacity. I interacted only informally and refused to give anything on record as I was not authorized to do so.

Revenue Recovery

The Revenue Recovery and action against illegal transfer of land remained to be completed. Since I had to pursue the Revenue Recovery aspect of the Company, I needed to get hold of the details regarding its assets. As mentioned earlier, the office files had no information about the Company.

My friend, in the India Revenue Service was posted as Asstt. Commissioner Income Tax in Kozhikode. So I got him to dig out the returns of the Company which would give further details. Next, I logged on to the MCA21 website of the Ministry of Company Affairs which had the database of all companies. Based on the returns and the details that I got from the MCA21 website, I drafted a letter to be sent by the Collector to the Registrar of Companies, Kochi requiring certain authenticated, certified information regarding the nature and holding of the Company. Within a week's time I had all the relevant data and it was interesting as well.

The Company had an outstanding arrear of approximately Rs. 39 lakhs towards Sales Tax and Rs. 29 lakhs towards Workmen's compensation. The Company refused to pay this despite Revenue Recovery (RR) through revenue recovery proceedings. A small part of the company land was attached in 2002. Nobody took that land in auction, and subsequently, the land was brought to Government ownership by paying a token amount of Re. 1. It is called 'bought-in-land'. (But such attachment is merely on paper and the Company would not care any less.) My Collector told me that such paper tigers will evoke no response from the Company. He suggested that I attach the best and most cardinal portion of the property. Finally, we decided to issue RR notice for the entire parcel of land.

Meanwhile, I got the banking details from Income Tax Department and the Company Registrar. The Bank accounts of the Company were frozen and steps were taken to attach the money in those accounts against the dues which are still not settled. But this could hardly meet the lakhs of rupees in arrear. Since the arrears were not fully met, Notice in Form 10 of Kerala Revenue recovery Act was issued for 11.8 acres of land now possessed by the Company. The Company did not respond. But on the last day, we got communication from the Labour Commissioner and the Sales Tax

Department that all dues were settled along with the collection charges due to the Revenue Department. Rs. 68 lakhs plus was settled at a single go. It was clear that the Company badly wanted that piece of land.

The Revenue Recovery part was also thus successfully completed.

Resuming the Land

This was the most difficult part as the decision was to be made at the government level and not at the District level. As mentioned, the files had nothing about the land in question except for their Survey numbers. We had to do some digging. The starting point regarding the land was the Village record. These were verified. The BTR (Basic Tax Register) extracts and Village Office records corresponding to the Survey numbers had some mention of an agreement entered into between the Government and the Company in 1963 and 1964 in the remarks column. Logically, a copy of the Agreement should have been with us, in the file. But this was not so. The Industries Department also said that they did not have a copy of the Agreement. The Revenue Divisional Office records were searched and the file that finally confirms any land acquisition was recovered. From that one copy of Agreement was finally discovered but it was partially destroyed and practically useless.

I went back to the village office records. The old crumbling village office records mentioned that the agreements had been published in the Government Gazette. I then searched for the Kerala Gazette of the particular years for the text of the agreement. The Kozhikode Archive did not have Gazettes before 1970 and this pertained to 1962-1964. To get such an old record through proper official channels would take ages. I remembered that in the State Central Library, Trivandrum, (where I used to visit as a student) there was a huge Archives Section. I then got one of my old classmates in Trivandrum to procure it from the State Central Library, Trivandrum. He faxed me the relevant pages of the Gazette. *I now had the agreement and the terms that covered the whole land deal.* I could build the case.

The case could be summarized thus:

> *An extent of 4.18 acres and 4.65 acres in* ***R.S.*** *17/1A and 18/1A3 was acquired for Best India Steel Company. In the*

Revenue records, the land is seen in joint ownership of the Company and the Government. The Kerala Gazette, May 1963 at page 3 gives the agreement entered into between the Company and the Government on 29th May, 1962, which stipulates the conditions subject to which the Company shall have possession over the land[1]. *An extent of additional land of 2.98 acres in* ***R.S. No. 16/1B*** *and 0.40 acres in* ***18/1A2*** *of Cheruvannur Village was also acquired. This land is also in the joint ownership of the Company and Government as per Village Office records. Similar conditions are stipulated for this land as well in the agreement, dated 27.5.1964 between the Company and the Government.*

The Company had held that they bought an additional 74 cents of land from private parties and the administration was under the impression that it was true and it was stated so in the Collectorate file. But when I checked the Village Office and Taluk Office records, 74 cents in ***18/1A4****, was found to be acquired by the government and placed in the joint ownership of the Company and the Government.*

The entire land of 12.95 acres possessed by the Company was thus acquired by the Government under Land Acquisition Act and placed in joint ownership of the Company and the Government. The agreements covering the entire parcel of land specifically prohibits any transfer or alienation of this land. The land was to be used only for the purpose of acquisition. Thus no other commercial operation could take place on the land.

As per records got from various sources mentioned earlier, the Company is a Non-Government company with registered office at Jhalum House, Kozhikode. 100 per cent equity is owned by the Directors or relatives of directors. The Government has no stake in the Company. The Company declared lock out in the year 1997. Yet in the financial year 2006-07 it declared a profit after tax of Rs. 66.34 lakhs as per records available with the Registrar of Companies. It is to be noted that for the past 11 years the company is not functioning and the land assigned to the Company is not used for the intended purpose. The profit declared by the Company, despite not functioning for the last 11 years clearly indicates that its source of income is elsewhere, i.e. leased out land.

This violated the agreement of 1964 that says:

Clause 4(b): "The land shall be used only for the purpose of establishing a Steel Re-rolling Mill Foundry and workshop and putting up other structures in connection therewith."
Clause 4(c): "The land shall not be alienated or encumbered or charged in any manner without the previous sanction in writing of the Government."

Clause 4(e) of the Agreement of 1964 is thus attracted:

"In the case of infringement of any of the above conditions or in the event of voluntary relinquishment of the land by the company or in the event of dissolution of the company or its extinction, the Government may resume the land........."

Similarly, ***Clause 3(c) of the Agreement of 1963*** is attracted:

"That in event of the company being wound up or in the event of failure on the part of the Company to carry out the terms of the agreement that is to say establishing of a Steel Re-rolling Mill, Foundry and Workshop for Messrs. Best India Steel Co, Private Ltd., Calicut the land shall be liable to be resumed and taken back by the said Government on repayment to the company of the amount of the award as finally settled less the 15 per cent awarded for the compulsory acquisition or the estimated market value of the land at the time of resumption whichever shall be less and if there are any buildings on the land, the Governor may at his option either purchase the buildings on payment of their estimated value at the time, or direct the company to remove the buildings at its own cost within such time as may be allowed by the said Government."

During the eviction process, Jhalum Motors Ltd. had submitted that they were functioning on the said land occupying 4.18 acres of the said land on the basis of an agreement entered into with Best India Steel Co. Ltd. dated 16.1.2006. This admission was now used against Best India Steel Co. This is violative of ***Section 45(A) of L.A. Act (Acquisition of land for Companies):***

> *"No Company for which any land is acquired under this part shall be entitled to transfer the said land or any part thereof by sale, mortgage, gift, lease or otherwise except with the previous sanction of the Government."*

The remedy for such violation of the terms of the agreement is resumption of the land by the Government. Therefore, a show cause notice dated 12.06.2008 was drafted which was issued by the Collector to the Company.

The reply given by Best India Steel Co. was far from satisfactory. It was claimed that the land leased out to Jhelum Motor Co. Ltd. was free of any restrictions. (They apparently did not know that we already had the documents covering every inch of the land) In the reply they admitted that Jhelum Motor Co. Ltd. had been permitted to utilize the land. Besides, letters received from Jhelum Motors Ltd. regarding the land encroachment issue under KLC Act clearly admitted that a 'leave and licence' agreement was entered into between both the Companies on 16th January, 2006. Amusingly, despite admitting all these violations, the reply filed by Best India Steel Co. Ltd. asserts that they did not violate any clauses of the agreement.

The reply appeared to be baseless and legally untenable, given the records available with us. The entire parcel of land covering a total extent of 11.8 acres in R.S. Nos.17/1A, 18/1A3, 16/1B, 18/1A2 and 18/1A4 is clearly and comprehensively covered by the Agreements of 1963 and 1964 with regard to the mode of utilization and transfer. Besides, Section 45A of the Land Acquisition Act also covers these lands. All the records in the Village Office and the Taluk Office, besides other legal records and documents support the Government position.

On 14th July, 2008, I completed the detailed Report on Best India Steel Co. Ltd., which was to be sent to the Principal Secretary, Revenue by the District Collector. This report was to give a detailed picture of the genesis and status of the whole issue. All the legal aspects were to be lucidly explained. The Collector requested that the Government may be pleased to issue orders to resume the land invoking ***Clauses 4(b), 4(c)*** and ***4(e)*** of the Agreement of 1964 and ***Clause 3(c)*** of the Agreement of 1963 read along with ***Section 45A*** of the Land Acquisition Act, without further delay, in the best interest of the State.

Based on this letter, the Secretary Revenue gave a hearing opportunity to the Company. On 6th November, 2008, I appeared before Mr. Deepak Gupta, Deputy Secretary (hearing the case for the Principal Secretary) representing the District Collector in the case of Best India Steel Co. Ltd. Our submission was that the land given to the Company was to be resumed and taken back by the Government since the agreement conditions stand violated. It was a nice experience to argue this case because Mr. Vivek Meron had engaged the best High Court lawyers on their side. Once I had produced the file before the Deputy Secretary with detailed flagging and evidence to prove every condition of violation, the Advocates seemed to be a bit surprised. They had not expected a professional and legally tidy case. We had collected all the relevant evidence, step by step and piece by piece. We procured relevant data about the Company from the Income Tax Department, Registrar of Companies, Panchayat records, etc., thereby buttressing the file and our arguments. The only way they could wriggle out, I believe, was by making the file disappear. The Advocates prayed for time. The case was posted for 22nd November, 2008. I again went to Trivandrum to argue the case. It was more of the lawyer in me who was getting excited with this case.

Their advocates brought out innovative but really fantastic arguments but they themselves knew that the game was up. As the case was being heard that day, a file came from the Industries Minister to the table of the Revenue Secretary. The advocate dramatically asked the Deputy Secretary to peruse that file as well before a decision was taken. It was about a project proposal submitted by the Company for revival. Since it was planning to 'restart' its operations, the Industries Department had been requested assistance from the side of the government. The purpose was to save the "jobs" of the workers of the Company. (All workers were laid off long back. Only 3, including the Director and clerical staff were left on the Company pay roll. The 'Detailed Project Report' had not one word about financing source for the 100 crore revival package.) On the file, the Secretary, Industries and the Minister had signed on the same day. (The day before the hearing was conducted). This was very cinematic!

The case was posted for orders.

Despite all the last-minutes dramatic performances the Secretary ruled in favour of the proposal sent by the District Collector. The file was sent to the minister for approval so that orders for resumption could be issued. The file has since been resting on the table of the Revenue Minister. The land resumption order never came out.

7

Entebbe and Kandahar

A Case in Hostage Negotiation

B. Ashok

1. Leadership and Strategic Capability

The hostage release operations at Entebbe (1976) and Kandahar (1999) are studies in contrast from the point of view of classic phases in hostage crises and the respective responses of the State actors. The strategic centrality of the hostage takers' demands is emphasized as the key dynamic that sets a series of option-searching and decision-making acts in motion. The various preconditioning factors determining the interests of hostage takers and State actors in the developing crises are traced out, in addition to an analysis of why the Indian response to Kandahar was operationally and strategically flawed, with a long-term impact on India's hostage doctrine.

2. Two Crises, Two Outcomes

July 4, 1976, and December 31, 1999, are crucial dates that changed the way two important democracies facing the most protracted and destructive territorial disputes (Palestine and Kashmir) respectively faced their 'moment of truth' with different strategies, styles, tactics, capabilities and end results. These divergent challenges, decisions and responses had dramatic and lasting impact on the two nations' counter-terror doctrines and on their popular psyche.

The first of these incidents ended in Entebbe in Uganda with the forced storming, extraction of hostages and execution of all directly involved terrorists by Israeli commandos.

The second ended in Kandahar in Afghanistan, marked by the negotiated release of hostages with the exchange of crucial previously arrested terrorist assets, including motivationally and doctrinally important leaders.

Both events deeply affected post-incident national attitudes: the first marked by dynamic optimism and progressive though prolonged negotiations towards a political solution for the underlying problem; the second tainted by low morale, open drift and weakness in the political leadership, escalated terrorist violence, including attacks on audaciously demonstrative targets such as the Indian Parliament using suicide squads, successful strikes at numerous chosen targets by militants, and a State of general pessimism, lack of confidence and indignity amongst the responding (security) community.

Both, therefore, were rare instances of crucial successes: one from a State's point of view and the other from an anti-State actor's point of view. Entebbe reflected the military and strategic supremacy of Israel, which could not possibly be regionally challenged any further, at that stage, by Palestinian capabilities; while Kandahar brutally reminded India that all its strength in conventional and strategic forces did not necessarily add up to overcome the leadership challenge which — combined with a series of real-time tactical errors characterized by an intensely risk averse and bureaucratic decision-making process, and by the extreme lack of accountability of systems — established a legacy of capitulation and extreme willingness to accept soft options. The Indian response demonstrated unambiguously that strategic goals tended to be ignored or pushed to the background by posturing and ephemeral, rhetorical, highly questionable and whimsical policies unfortunately thrust upon the nation arbitrarily.

Entebbe successfully demonstrated the effectiveness and reach of Israel's swift military capability. Kandahar once again exposed India's faction ridden political mosaic, incoherent and uncoordinated policing and public service system, weaknesses in in-country and foreign intelligence coordination, poor development of strategy and tactical apparatus, and, overall, an unaccountable and capricious leadership at the moment of crisis.

Worse, the manifest failures to arrive at timely decisions and the faulty decisions taken by senior executives and political leaders in India were never systematically examined *post facto* by any suitable public investigation, and no accountability was ever fixed. The 'lessons not learnt and refused to be learnt' further exposed India's aviation sector, which is a key national asset for terrorist takeovers and even catastrophic attacks like that on September 11, 2001.

This Chapter explores eight crucial aspects of the Entebbe and Kandahar crises and looks for learning points from the Israeli and Indian experience.

3. Aviation Hostage Crises in History

After the September 2001 attacks in New York, the issue of aviation security in the context of terrorist takeovers of civilian aircraft has assumed new significance. The 9/11 attack also marked a profound tactical departure from conventional hostage-taking, which was defensive, to the new and deadly combination of human shields, using aircraft fuselages as missiles, huge quantities of aviation fuel as warheads, and the tactical choice of high visibility targets, to enhance the damage potential to the level of weapons of mass destruction.

The first wave of hijackings in the post-Second World War era was mostly done by convicts or refugees escaping from communist countries, or political dissenters, fleeing hostile regimes. An analysis of all hijacking incidents since 1947 shows that 61 per cent of these were committed to facilitate refugee escapes.[1] Hijackings exploded between 1968 and 1969, at the peak of the Cold War — nuclear deterrence was, paradoxically, threatening civil aviation security. In 1969, there were 82 hijack attempts in the World, more than the total number of attempts in the preceding two decades between 1947 and 1967.[2] After 1968, a majority of hijackings were executed by US's criminals fleeing for Cuba or in attempts to escalate the Israel-Palestinian conflict, where terrorists used hijacking as a political weapon to publicize their cause and to secure release of key Palestinian terrorist assets from prisons.

The anti-Hijack measures initiated in the US from 1973 and diplomatic initiatives such as the US-Cuba hijack pact substantially reduced hijacks after the 1967-1976 period, when total incidents peaked, with 385 events world wide.[3] Between 1977 and 1986, the phenomenon declined, with 200 incidents, a level roughly maintained in the succeeding decade, with 212 incidents between 1987 and 1996.[4]

Between 1980 and 1990, however, terrorists shifted attention to larger transport aircraft as 'stunt terrorism' targets. The Air India bombing in 1985 near Canada and the Pan American bombing over Lockerbie (UK) in 1988 demonstrated this trend. However, hostage-hijacks continued as an instrument to coerce State actors to give concessions to prisoners. The TWA hijack to Beirut in 1989 and the Kuwait Airways hijack of 1988 were successful from the terrorist point of view. On the other hand, the December 1994 hijacks by the armed Algerian Islamic Group (GIA) resulted in French Gendarmerie storming the aircraft and releasing all passengers and troops in Marseilles.

When suicide hijackers gain control of an aircraft, it is critical that the information regarding its flight path and possible target or destination is conveyed as rapidly as possible to crisis decision makers and that air traffic control, civilian and military authorities coordinate all emergency action. Post 9/11, aircraft have become potential WMDs. Countries like France have deployed surface to air missiles around key political targets to provide swifter responses than interception by fighter aircraft. Countries including India are also establishing 'no fly zones' and well rehearsed plans to prevent 'suicide sabotage' scenarios. With these, combined with a high degree of boarding gate and in-flight security, aviation experts hope to contain the challenge.

An interesting technological innovation which would prevent purposeful sabotage is a computer programme called Robolander which will allow the ground air traffic controller to override the manual aircraft landing system and land the craft safely, despite manifest control by the pilot, thus avoiding the incentive for the Hijackers to harm passengers or pilots. Adoption of this system will, however, be time-consuming and demands a high degree of international coordination and standardization. The chance of the ATC itself becoming the target of hijack, subterfuge and takeover cannot, moreover, be ruled out once such a system is established.

4. The Kinetics of Entebbe and Kandahar

Both Entebbe and Kandahar invalve all the classic phases of an aviation hostage crisis. Though separated by more than twenty three years in time, and by radical intervening changes in the polarity of global political arrangements, a quantum jump in military hardware, the digitization of signals and warfare, internet and more sophisticated satellite and human intelligence systems, they broadly conform to established patterns in the tricks, tactics and strategies of a hostage taker.

5. Centrality and Dynamics of Objective and Aggressors' Demand

The primary attribute of the hostage taker/hijacker is the absolute clarity of his/her objective and stake in the process. The sophisticated scheming and tactics adopted by them follows a doctrine which is established at fairly high levels of the terror organization's hierarchy. The strategic objective of the Entebbe hostage takers, the People's Liberation Front of Palestine (PLFP) and the Kandahar hijackers, the Harkat-ul-Mujahideen (HuM) with the support of the Inter-Services Intelligence (ISI), Pakistan's external intelligence agency, was to secure the release of some of their key leadership and operatives jailed in the States fighting the terrorist organizations.

The Entebbe incident involved Flight 139, an Air France Jet carrying 256 passengers and 12 crew members, flying from Tel Aviv through Athens to Paris. Here, the hijackers demanded the release of about 50 terrorist leaders and supporters jailed in many countries, including Israel, France and Kenya. In retrospect, by this tactical blunder in demanding an internationally unattainable objective, the hijackers forced Israel to seriously consider, plan and finally execute the military operation at Entebbe. The successful IC 814 hijacking involved an Indian Airlines plane with 178 passengers and 11 crew members aboard. In this case, the hijackers exhibited great flexibility and political awareness to narrow their tactical objective down to the release of just three key militants jailed within their target country, India, down from the release of 36 terrorists originally demanded. The hijackers also showed willingness to drop two possibly difficult demands — the recovery of the dead body of a terrorist and demands for a ransom (Stated at US$ 200 million), in addition to tactical concessions exchanged with national authorities during the flights interim halt at Dubai (release of some women and some children for food and fuel). With military support from the then Taliban regime in Afghanistan, and overt support from the ISI, eventual negotiated settlement ended the game very much on the hijackers' terms.

The lesson for all future possible hijackers from the limited and precise nature of the HuM demands is that demands which tend to be successful have a borderline status of possible political acceptability, with the target Government being able to make an explicit case that the outcome does not amount to a major setback or an outright military defeat. Demands, consequently, need more than amateur consideration; they need to be weighed for tactical superiority, objective, morale, possibility of compliance by the State actor, and flexibility to scale down to essentials. The demands should never be set at a level that compels military action as the only option left for key decision-maker in the target country. The outcome must be politically marketable, and must not cross the threshold into a 'no go' situation, forcing a radical military response. Steeper demands can only be supported with much weightier stakes, such as VIP hostages or WMD, to force the target State to play the game on the terrorists' terms.

6. Choice of Space and Time

In both Entebbe and Kandahar, the hijackers used a third territory, where the threat perception to stage and board the aircraft was lower. In the Entebbe case, Athens was much less guarded as a target airport and the metal detector was not even manned. The hijackers showed initiative and imagination in striking at the point of least resistance. For Entebbe, the four 'muscle hijackers' — two Arabs and two terrorists for hire who were German nationals — transferred in transit from Singapore Airline flight 763 from Bahrain. In the IC 814 case, which ended at Kandahar, the transfer of five hijackers was from a Pakistan International Airlines (PIA) aircraft again through transit at Kathmandu. In this critical event at Kathmandu, the complicity of an ISI officer has been established beyond doubt by local authorities.[5] However, some complicity of the security details in Kathmandu cannot be ruled out. In addition to the hand guns and Kalashnikovs the hijackers brandished at onset of the crisis, they also subsequently accessed a large cache of ammunition stowed in the baggage hold of the aircraft, once the flight landed at Kandahar.

Flight 139 was hijacked immediately after departure from Athens. Flight IC 814 was hijacked after a short delay, about twenty minutes into the flight, after entering Indian territory. The hijackers waited tactically for the cockpit hatch to be opened for beverage services so establishing control over the pilots could be easier. Both takeovers were rapid: less than a minute long and executed very quickly, with full coordination, precision and role clarity. Kinetic analysis reveals repeated rehearsals. Hijackers typically sprung to the aisles and brandished weapons, attacked some closer passengers with bare hands or the butt of weapons and ensured that the entire passenger cabin received the shocking message loud and clear. It is likely that the hijackers rehearsed this phase repeatedly, since the potential for resistance or violence at this point during the crisis tends to be at a maximum.

Neutralizing any potential resistance at the very beginning, if necessary, by hurting a passenger or two who show poor or late compliance to orders, is a stunning tactic used by many hijackers. Subjugation to the fear of brandished weapons and taking cover from possible bodily hurt is the key theme in the minds of the hostages and they barely think about the medium term outcome or finale of the unfolding drama. The tactical objective of hijackers is to dominate the aisles and segregate passengers, with military-aged males (MaMS) securely tied up and at close gunpoint. In most instances, they are the first targets of 'humane' execution.

7. Choice of Staging for Negotiation

The first onset phase usually ends with the hijackers securing and positioning the craft and hostages for negotiation and easy selective targeting, in case they resort to execution. Family members are segregated from each other and males, females and children seated separately. By the time the craft is positioned or stabilized, the key issue in the demands would be exchanged between the hostages and negotiators or/and State party involved. In this phase, the hijackers would vehemently try to evade the State party's territory, particularly after the well publicized positioning of anti-hijack squads in striking distance from most important civil airports in strategic locations. In the Entebbe case, the hijackers, with the help of their political masters, chose Libya and Uganda as successive interim locations, where no hostility to their political cause was to be expected. Landing in Libya was planned for refuelling. The Libyan, Pakistani (Lahore) and Dubai leaderships behaved similarly. They allowed refuelling and replenishment of food and cleaning, but refused to entertain the other demands, such as extended stay. The choice of Uganda under dictator Idi Amin, who helped the Palestinian hijackers overtly, and of the Kandahar, where the anti-Indian hijackers expected and promptly received military, logistical and political support from the Taliban, with whom India was yet to establish any diplomatic relationship after their take-over of the country in 1996, demonstrate this point. Israel also had no direct diplomatic relations with Uganda and Amin's enmity to Israel and his support to the Palestinian cause at that time was well known.

8. Stabilization Phase

Once the *status quo* between the hijackers and the hostages is established and the rules of engagement are clear to both parties, the hijack could be considered to be stabilized or poised for resolution or escalation, depending on the next strategic moves by the actors. The instances under present analysis entered the phase of stabilization as soon as the craft touched down in Entebbe and the hostages were secured in the old terminal block there; and, in the Indian case, as they were securely held in the cold aircraft on the Kandahar tarmac, freed from any risk of assault from Indian Forces. This phase demonstrated the clear domination of, and control of the tactical initiative by the hijackers. They held the bargaining chips the option of declaring and altering the deadlines and specific threats of execution of or harm to hostages at frequent intervals.

The idea is to allow domestic pressure on the hostage community to escalate and counter-balance the apparent political inconvenience of the decisions demanded. Deadlines of less than 24 hours are counter productive here. Sufficient time is allowed for media to expand the story as well as concentrate attack on the State actors, usually for their presumed indecision and inaction. Since there is no exigency on their part on account of immediate threat and since they are well defended by friendly national troops, the key choice left before the State actor is to choose between negotiated processes or the option of military force. Apart from debating the particular concessions sought, this is the central dilemma of the State actor in any air hostage crisis. The constraints on State actors in such cases include the total lack of control in the territory where stabilization has been engineered, possible problems with international law of aggression, and air traffic access; and the potential of full casualty, which may domestically be perceived as a political and military defeat.

9. The Non-choice of No-negotiation

There are two negotiation models in vogue (1) the US/Israel professed model of no negotiations with terrorists; and (2) the pragmatic model of talking formally to avoid/delay harm, and simultaneously explore force or political options, as frequently adopted by India and many other countries. The engagement of negotiators is however inevitable in either case. Even US and Israel negotiate through the national party in the holding territory or through third parties, at least for the level of logistics and supplies. Entirely cutting off communications with the craft or the hijackers is never an option, since they can always easily sacrifice a token hostage to force the reopening of the doors of negotiation or take even more drastic actions.

Once negotiators from, or representing, the target country are positioned and engaged, the onus of problem solving shifts to the target country. The highest executive authority will have to consider the often politically damaging demands, while the military option may resurface if a credible plan is offered and mounted at this stage. Here, the military leadership, if consulted right from the beginning, can explore windows of professional opportunity.

One clear rule to be kept in mind, from classic negotiation theory is that the negotiators mandate must be fixed hourly or even more frequently by the political advisers and key functionaries in charge. The force option, if planned, must not be known at all to the negotiators. If the storming is planned it must be done by a separate team and the principal negotiator must be given the mandate of distracting the lead terrorist. Before the storming action is initiated, no word of it must even be contemplated in the negotiation room. Even the slightest hint of the option of force being explored in the voice or tenor of the negotiator can provoke a catastrophic ending.

Clearly, in both the Entebbe and the Kandahar instances, the stabilization phase started on day three and four, respectively. In the Israeli case, the hijackers exchanged French and non-Israeli passengers for food and services, met the demanded release of some other hostages and also set a 48 hours first deadline. In Kandahar also, after December 27, 1999, a little too late according to some observers, the civilian team led by an Indian diplomat engaged the hijackers in negotiations and finalized the demand for release of three terrorists, leaving roughly 72 hours for the Indian Government to consider all their options. Both aircrafts and hostages remained in captivity for almost eight days, Indians reaching freedom on the eve of the millennial New Year in Delhi.

The reason why Israel considered the military operation early and actively can be attributed to its freshly sanguinary history as a targeted nation; a persistent hostage and victim consciousness, which prompts retaliation; a strong resonance of the harsh memories of the holocaust; and a determination in the political leadership that the horrors of the past would never be repeated at any costs, (As the then highest ranking officer of the IDF expressed it, "What good is Israel if Israelis are selected and slaughtered?");[6] and the early realization that the demands of the hijackers were unrealistic, amateurish and practically impossible to meet.

It was, interestingly, the Israeli Defence Minister Shimon Peres who asked the Chief of Staff, Motuhai Motu Gaur, to prepare "the plans he did not have". While General Gaur had initially recommended a negotiated political settlement, Prime Minister Yitzhak Rabin and Peres, who were political rivals by that time, with Peres known to be eyeing the chair of the Prime Minister, had detected the infeasibility of the political concessions the hijackers had demanded.[7] This gave considerable committed time for making an 'impossible' rescue mission possible. The Entebbe mission has, of course, since become a staple of instructions in military schools for its precision, preparation, actionable, sharp and clear intelligence, leadership, sacrifice, surprise and technical prowess, even in that age of analog technology.

10. Key Gaps in the Indian Response

In Kandahar case, there was also a lag-time for the Indian response system to get its act together. Though the signal intimating the hijacking of the aircraft was available to the Delhi ATC at 4.40 pm on December 24, the Crisis Management Committee chaired by the Cabinet Secretary seems neither to have met nor communicated with candidate response airports, where the plane could be landing, in the succeeding two hours.[8] Since the origin of the aircraft was Kathmandu, and since the ATC radar gave indications that it was moving North-Westwards, just two options were available, in the order of increasing gravity and risk. One was to identify the candidate airports the hijackers might choose and get at least local authority and force staged there, with a clear mandate, or at least sufficient forewarning. Why the cabinet crisis system failed to specify the mandate of local authorities (meaning the District Collector and Superintendent of Police/Commissioner/Inspector General of Police) of Ahmedabad, Amritsar, Mumbai or Jammu till 6.04 pm, when it was clear that Amritsar was to be the staging area, is not clear. At 6.04 pm, Amritsar received the aircraft's landing signals.

Clearly, the bureaucratic establishment did not conduct the basic intellectual exercise of projecting the possible destinations. Worse, despite the Cabinet Secretary being present in New Delhi, there were no orders available to the Amritsar local authority for the 40 minutes the aircraft stayed on tarmac. In fact, the Director General of Punjab Police was not contacted at all; he was left to collect the news from Television at 6.00 pm, by his own admission.[9] That reflects also on his poor intelligence coordination. New Delhi was clearly out of character as a national capital responding to a national emergency: nobody assumed responsibility in these crucial two hours after which the Captain of IC 814 was forced to fly off across national borders to Lahore in Pakistan. The Flight Captain was the only one in charge from the Indian side at that point.

It was at 6.40 pm that New Delhi told Amritsar to delay refuelling as far as possible — the first signs of life in Delhi's crisis ridden crisis management system. By this time, however, a decision for a no-decision could no longer be enforced — since the hijackers had started killing hostages. One hostage was mortally wounded and later died, upon which the pilot, was forced to take off at 7.45 pm. It was at the stage of intentional delay that the second option could have become operational, when a late decision in New Delhi, conveyed to the team in Amritsar, sought to instruct Punjab Police Commandos to shoot and deflate the tires of the AB 300 aircraft, which the local team had some training for. But this could have provoked direct retaliation from the hijackers in terms of the killing of more hostages, or even of the pilots, or a finale in total disaster. The reasoning in the New Delhi analyst's mind was to prevent the aircraft being taken to hostile territory. But without a concomitant storming, neutralization and extraction plan (which Amritsar had executed successfully in 1994 against a lone, less trained, hijacker) this was a non-starter. In retrospect, the solitary act of disabling the tyres would have been extremely counter-productive in the absence of an effective plan for neutralizing the hijackers.

This raises the key question, why was the storming decision not left to the local authorities at Amritsar, who could have acted legally under the mandate of the District Magistrate, provided the local capabilities existed? It is now known that New Delhi wanted the NSG commandos to take on the storming, but they failed to reach Amritsar before the aircraft took off for Lahore at 7.45 pm. These failures indicate a key strategic and operational gap in New Delhi's response system. Given three hours and five minutes of lead time, it is astonishing that New Delhi could not decide and mount a commando operation in a city as close as Amritsar. This was at least six times off the standard of NSG's stated response standard of 30 minutes. The other stark deficiency in India's response to Amritsar was the total absence of military planners or of the Army or Air Force in mounting the response. In retrospect, even the then Home Minister and Defence Minister traded charges, each claiming that they were not adequately consulted, and that the Foreign Ministry monopolized the response, especially during the stabilization phase. Clearly, the Cabinet Secretariat and Home Ministry, along with civil aviation controllers (the Civil Aviation Safety Bureau) failed to remain in full communication, compare options, predict outcomes and mount a quick response. Worse, we have no evidence that any of the airports in the episode had a quick response Force back-up which is airlifted and actionable even after 1999, like the successful *Groupe d'Intervention de la Gendarmerie Nationale* (GIGN, the French counter-terrorism unit) which stormed the hijacked Air France aircraft successfully at Marseilles in 1994.

Further, there was no readiness to involve the operational command of the Air Force or alert the Army, since the civilian establishment was clearly determined to handle this key development alone, with far-reaching consequences, when handled as a police crisis. The Defence Ministry was almost entirely out of the picture from beginning to end, except for Cabinet-level discussions. There is hardly anything in the public domain even now, to determine whether the Army, which had sufficient paratroopers and aircraft,.was preparing an operational plan in those four crucial days — forget rehearsals or execution, for rescue and extraction, if needed, in Kandahar.

The fact of the matter was the Indian Army did not have the ready capacities for operational force projection beyond its western frontier, in a remote locale like Kandahar. The country had neither set superior ambitions nor trained extensively in trans-border operations in the near abroad. The Force had entirely missed tactical transformation, beyond sporadic acquisitions, which were themselves bogged down by logistic and corruption linked quagmires. Even Army lacked neither operable plans nor a feasible extraction unit which could storm and retrieve the passengers, even with collateral damage. Caught in a fight for survival on the country's borders and the Kashmir Valley, ambient, offensive, city specific 'dupstrike' capabilities simply did not exist, despite the availability of necessary technologies.

In sharp contrast, at Entebbe, the military and not the domestic crisis team handled the problem right from the beginning. With the Israeli Defence Force Chief sitting in Cabinet, the viability of a distant and risky operation was always present before the decision makers. The distance of Force commanders from key decision-making bodies and their replacement by civilian foreign policy experts and civilian negotiators cost India dearly in the final count.

India's diplomacy-based plan in the negotiations at Kandahar was also flawed in its basic assumptions, right from the beginning.

The Foreign Service officer, who led the team comprising internal and external security experts, as well as his political leaders, were convinced that India had considerable concessions to offer the Taliban, and hence some leverage. They, for instance, regarded recognition of the Taliban regime by India as a major concession. The diplomat's team was very skeptical about the Taliban offering any hard on-site cooperation in exchange for unilateral recognition, and this, in fact, is exactly what happened. Leverage just did not exist. Neither could sufficient track-two pressure be exerted by the covert establishment to elicit cooperation from the Taliban. India was playing for high stakes without any cards to back the gamble. Concessions of a monetary nature to the Taliban would have been fully justified to neutralize their response, particularly to secure the withdrawal of their offensive armoured vehicles which had been deployed visibly to pre-empt Indian forces from storming of the craft. The option of neutralizing the defensive Taliban Force guarding the aircraft was not explored at all.

11. The Final Faux Pax

Finally, the negotiators established working relationships with the hijackers and succeeded in eking some concessions. They had started working through stable communications and, with Taliban mediation, secured some key results from the hijackers, when New Delhi did the final *volte face*, unilaterally accepting all the hijackers' demands at one go. This is known to have been a decision that surprised everyone in the loop, including the negotiators. The perception was that it came at a moment when the situation had stabilized and pressure was building on the hostage takers to offer further counter-concessions. Assessments suggest that India could have retained two of the 'target assets' out of the three demanded, when New Delhi abruptly and dramatically gave up the battle of wits.

A controversial unilateral decision was taken, allegedly at the highest level, to accede to all the remaining demands at once, and arrangements were made to release the key targets of the terrorists' demands, including Maulana Mazood Azhar, from Kot Balwal jail in Jammu, where he was lodged. The express reason: the functionary did not want hostages "to spend New Year in captivity".[10]

One express rule in such negotiation under duress is that the stressor must have full discretion in setting all deadlines. Setting arbitrary and external deadlines is suicidal in terms of outcome, since this forecloses the possibility of further reductions of the aggressor's targets.

Maulana Masood Azhar was flown to New Delhi by a RAW jet and transferred to an IA aircraft in which the External Affairs Minister Jaswant Singh escorted the terrorist ideologue and two other 'terrorist assets' — Mushtaq Ahmed Zargar and Ahmed Omar Saeed Sheikh — to Kandahar.[11] While one camp in the establishment justified this act of the Foreign Minister, as a caring and sensitive gesture towards the super-stressed hostages, which also helped contain the pressures on the Government exerted by the families of the hostages, the move was widely portrayed as capitulation of the highest order. This, indeed, was Masood Azhar's subsequent and vehement projection in Pakistan.

Home Minister L.K. Advani, who had criticized both the Rubaiya Saeed episode, when V. P. Singh was Prime Minister,[12] as well as the trading of food with hostage-takers at Hazratbal,[13] was not in agreement with the final decision on Kandahar. It would later transpire that the hijackers' tactical objective in insisting on the Foreign Minister accompanying the released terrorists was intended to pre-empt any possible Indian misadventure, such as crashing the plane carrying the key terrorist assets. In effect, the presence of the Minister completely ruled out the force option.

It was also lost on the Indian covert establishment to plant a satellite linkable transponder to the persons of the released hostages, in order to locate and recapture or eliminate through a retaliatory strike by a crack team after a few hours of the flight's return to safety. It is not known whether such a capability existed at that time, or whether such capabilities have even been acquired today.

In stark contrast, the Israeli commandos had the forethought to destroy the radar at Entebbe and the few jets that Idi Amin had, in case they pursued the rescue aircraft.

12. The Termination Model

The classic termination phase described in the literature on such crises also throws light on the Entebbe and Kandahar cases. While the negotiators successfully or unsuccessfully manipulated the relationships developed through the standoff phase, the termination follows the acceptance of negotiated settlements or, in their absence, the exercise of the force option.

There are only three logical real world outcomes:

1. Partial or full acceptance of demands/hijackers surrenders peacefully and are arrested and tried.
2. Force option: Police/commandos storm the craft and kill, maim or arrest hijackers with or without harm to hostages.
3. Partial or full acceptance of demands and hijackers are given some lead time for escape, with complicity of the host country and they disappear to live in safe havens, which are pre-negotiated with host or State party.

In any eventuality, the onset phase and the termination phase hold maximum risk for the hostages, and it is in these phases that maximum casualties are recorded. The Entebbe operation, which took 72 hours of planning and an imperfect Sinai desert exercise for night landing, which was a limited success, left four dead and one seriously injured. The commander of the Israel Defence Force raiders, Lt. Col. Yonatan Netanyahu, and three hostages were killed. Nevertheless, the Israelis and the world accept the operation as a total and exemplary success, and these sacrifices were perceived as necessary for the objectives achieved. In other words, the operation reduced a near total damage scenario to fewer than 3 per cent casualties, a proportion entirely acceptable and politically saleable domestically, when balanced with the huge strategic and political success at Entebbe. Collateral damage was overwhelmingly balanced out by the doctrinal and political gains. The real criterion of success is the strategic and political balance secured through the end game.

To India's credit, it may be said that it chose wisely to concede just one casualty — that too, in the onset phase, and in a chance event. From the perspective of lives saved, the chosen option was a near-total success. In hindsight, however, the political and material costs of the release of dreaded and potentially highly destructive fanatical motivational leaders proved very costly. The complicity of Saeed Sheikh in the 9/11 attacks in the US and the Daniel Pearl killing, and of Masood Azhar's group — Jaish-e-Mohammed — in the attack on India's

Parliament in December 2001, and in a rash of lesser, but devastating terrorist operations in Jammu and Kashmir and other parts of India, imposed an enormous strategic cost in India and beyond — a price that is still being paid. In one estimate, the loss of some 2,500 lives was attributed to direct acts of Azhar's outfit, just between 2000 and 2003.[14]

13. The Aftermath of Kandahar

The US stance at the time of the Kandahar crisis was repeatedly critiqued by Indian leaders. The US apparently sought to dissuade from undertaking any military operation on Afghan soil, as Washington was then hoping to develop military and commercial relations with a 'moderate Taliban'. Post 9/11, it dismantled its oil pipeline plans for *Unocal*, a US oil giant, and went all out after Taliban, who were then harbouring Osama bin Laden. At that time, however, US inaction and failure to assist India politically and logistically in its moment of great need discredited Washington in the eyes of Indian strategic planners, for a considerable period of time. It is only now, after the renewed nuclear agreement and deepening cooperation on a range of other issues that the quality of the relationship has been somewhat restored.

The strategic and tactical edge the IC 814 hijackers maintained throughout the operation needs special mention. The involvement of an immediate relative of one of the terrorist assets whose release they were demanding made the effort very emotional and direct (Mazood Azhar's brother, Ibrahim Azhar, was one of the hijackers). The hijackers were able to pressure the onset and standoff phases effectively, and secure a termination at a port of their choice, and with local defence preventing any adventurism by any potential aggressor. The exit route they had pre-negotiated with the Taliban, with the support of Pakistan's Inter Services Intelligence (they had an *iftar* party in Kandahar before being driven across to Quetta, capital of the Balochistan province in Pakistan) was also ingenious. Some observers believe that it was the convenience of the exit routes that prompted the successive choice of Dubai, Lahore and Kandahar as target ports for the hijackers.

As a near-total failure of its internal security apparatus and the exercise of the use of force option, Kandahar should have sent India's strategic planners back to their drawing tables. It established a precedent for future Governments to follow a weak 'negotiations and selective release of assets', even as it exposed deep infirmities in the Force capabilities of the purported 'regional hegemon'. India was seen to be a slow, pliant, elephantine giant, with a soft underbelly of uncrystallized political expression, poor civil-military coordination, deeply distrustful of empowering strategic military assets, of involving them in decision-making, and coordination with paratroopers, commandos and Force transport systems.

Terrorists are bound to exploit the windows of opportunity created by this, the fragmented civilian leadership, and uncoordinated intelligence and Force capabilities, to further their objectives in future as well.

The 'path of least resistance' response to the Kandahar crisis did have one positive consequence: the Indian Penal Code was amended to make the death sentence mandatory for any convicted future hijackers.

14. Conclusion

The Kandahar and Entebbe episodes, in sharp contrast, demonstrate the distinguishing absence of relevant and effective strategic and tactical leadership in India. The Israeli national leadership at the time averaged the age of 50; the Entebbe mission was executed by a team which averaged an age of 30. India's far two traditional leadership, having stuck in around for far too long, was in no hurry to prove anything. For them, there were no legacies to be left in the fight for survival.

The leadership factor could become much more crucial in the foreseeable future, with India behaving like a tottering giant, with poor coordination and dexterity in manoeuvering across the troubled and muddied waters of the simmering extremist and fundamentalist politics of South Asia. It is imperative that the leadership factor is addressed by intense capacity building across services and calling in the security apparatus for responding well to emergent situations, especially after the experience of the Mumbai attacks. The need to expose the intensely secretive covert apparatus in order to hold them accountable is also evident.

NOTES

1. Paul Wilkinson, *Terrorism* versus *Democracy : The Liberal* State *Response,* p. 161, London: Frank Cass, 2001.
2. *Ibid.*
3. *Ibid.*
4. *Ibid.*
5. Praveen Swami, "Bowing to Terrorism," *Frontline*, Chennai, Vol. 17, No. 01, January 8-21, 2000.
6. 'Operation Black Thunder' movie by Eyal Sher.
7. O.P. Sabharwal, *The Killer Instinct*, p. 109, Delhi: Rupa, 2000.
8. Swami, *Frontline*, Vol. 17, No. 01, January 8-21, 2000.
9. *Ibid.*
10. IC 814 Film, © National Geographic.
11. Swami, *Frontline*, Vol. 17, No. 01, January 8-21, 2000.
12. The then Union Home Minister Mufti Mohammad Saeed's daughter, Rubaiya Saeed, was abducted by militants of the Jammu & Kashmir Liberation Front (JKLF) on 1989. The negotiated release of the extremists was seen a surrender to the anti-terror actions by the State police forces and has since contributed to the weakening of anti-terror doctrine.
13. The Hazratbal mosque considered very holy for Islam for its association with the Prophet's relic, has come under periodic siege from Islamic terror agents. The 2001 efforts to negotiate with the terrorists holed up in the Mosque, rations were sent in by the authorities. The opposition critiqued this heavily.
14. Praveen Swami, "The Kandahar Plot," *Frontline*, Vol. 20, No. 24, November 22-December 5, 2003.

8

Dalit Inclusion in Local Self Governments

Madurai

B. Ashok and *Darez Ahamed*

Abstract

The violent discriminatory repression of Indian *dalits* (Scheduled Castes and Tribes) is a tragic reality which the republican Constitution of India could not fully solve in sixty years of operation. The numerous protective and promotional measures enshrined in the Constitution and spelt out in Acts of Parliament have been insufficient in implementation to meet the repressive practices in its entirety.

The Local Self-Government laws providing for proportional representation was seen by many as a means of grassroots level empowerment of the *dalits* by channelling State action for development. Field assessment by officers of the Indian Administrative Service in training prove that the constitutional mirage are far from being realized in the vitiated culture-custom complex the rural milieu is stuck in.

Field studies in Madurai district of Tamil Nadu, a south Indian State noted for its backward classes led State level political circus reveals new forces operating to realize the *dalit* cause. Committed administration from an impartial agency administering representation is as crucial as the law-making in this respect. At the same time the contributions of civil society, committed political mobilization and self-reliance of *dalit* groups is playing an important part.

"We know you find
Everything
About us ugly

To stand at our shoulder
Makes you small
And to see us shoulder to shoulder
Knits your brows

....

Look!
Look out of
Your fortress shut tight
The ice is melting
The foals are snorting
Bullocks chew sunlight
And Ekalavya is burnishing
Old rusted arrows
In the fire"

Malkan Singh (1996) in 'Listen Brahmin'

1. Introduction

The *dalits* of India are victims of centuries of forced exclusion from public socio-economic sphere. Termed the Scheduled Castes (SCs) since the India Act of 1935 listed them out, they have been generally reduced to performing menial tasks in the economy considered unclean and unworthy by the upper caste Hindus. Post-independence and the republican Constitution of 1950, the State has invested in several public policies aiming to end discrimination and promote education and health services in these communities. Notwithstanding these well meaning efforts, the condition of the SCs has not improved dramatically.

At the heart of their discontent with Indian development is the forced disempowerment and exclusion from social sphere including institutions like public service and judicial system. Organized crime is used to suppress their legitimate political aspirations. Analysis of prosecutions against upper caste individuals who transgressed the Prevention of Atrocities Act (1989) (Table 8.1 and Fig. 8.1) would show disturbing trends in the period 1981-1991, with an all time high of 16,000 registered cases in 1984-85. The trend has shown a dramatic decline since 1995, by almost 50 per cent. It is curious to note that this period also marks the rise of mass based SC movements in the Indian polity and the attempts to promote local self-governments as means of participation and empowerment.

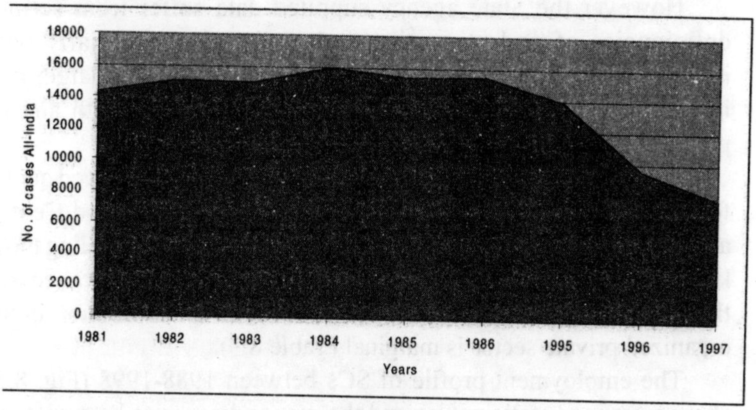

Fig. 8.1

Table 8.1: Crime Statistics for Crimes against SC/ST's in Tamil Nadu

Year	*Total (IPC+SLL)*	*IPC*	*SLL (PCR)*	*SLL (PAO)*	*Madurai District total*	*% share*	*Ranking in State by Number*	*Ranking in Crime Rate*
2005	1219	368	12	839	135	11	1	1
2004	1183	414	71	698	72	6.1	4	1
2003	1562	578	202	782	57	3.6	Na	1
2002	926 (excluding IPC)	NA	2	924	72	7.78	2	1
2001	840 (excluding IPC)	NA	11	829	86	10.24	2	1
2000	1028 (excluding IPC)	NA	38	996	72	7.2	2	1

SLL = Special and Local Laws.

PCR = Protection of Civil Rights Act, 1955.

POA = Prevention of Attrocities Act, 1989.

Fig. 8.2 depicts further evidence to the prevailing problems of State action against untouchability. Graph reveals a hundred fold increases in the number of cases registered under various sections of this penal law especially from 1970 till 1990. However, in the last six years where data is available, the trend has declined by one order of magnitude again, reflecting the positive social churning on.

However the State agency supplied data suffer from serious deficiencies of underreporting and moderation especially with inconvenient figures, and as a rule one must anticipate larger real incidence. Refusal to record first information reports with and by police is also very common.

While caste based affirmative actions in the form of reserved quotas for legislatures at all levels — Parliament to Panchayat, and Central and State government job reservations at 22.5 per cent (including those kept apart for the most underdeveloped Scheduled Tribes) have secured their participation in polity and government, their contribution in the organized private sector is marginal (Table 8.3).

The employment profile of SCs between 1988-1998 (Fig. 8.3) show entrapped static nature and the preponderance to be employed with rural based transient employment and as a result they suffer from higher incidence of deprivation among all employment categories.

While protective legislations like the Prevention of Atrocities Act are in force to prevent exploitation and harassment of the labouring masses, their flagrant violation and abuse are widely reported (Thorat, 2002). *Dalit* assertion of rights and friction in enforcing the basic of these are not uncommon in many Indian States. There are scholars who view the enlargement of the insurgencies towards self rule now manifest in about 175 Indian districts (of a total of 611) is a direct anarchy from this explicit suppression of the *dalits* rights and low opportunity for self-development.

2. New Tensions

In the realm of inclusive and socially just development, the North Indian and South Indian States show marked differences in approaches and results. While States like Kerala, Tamil Nadu, Karnataka, Andhra Pradesh and Maharashtra have been proactive in their inclusive

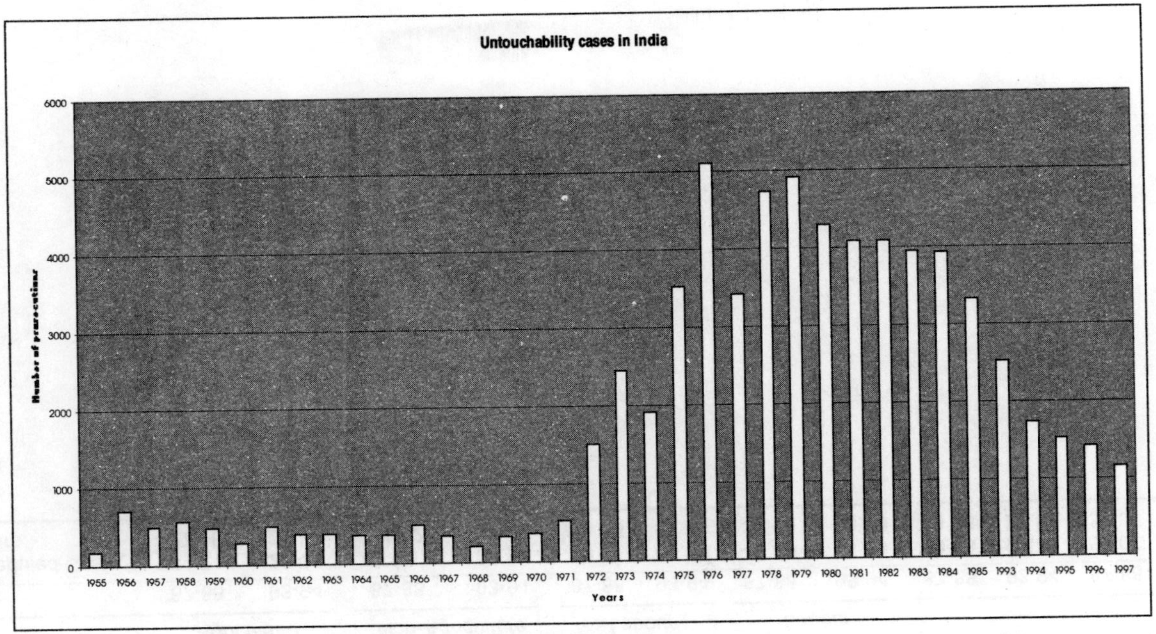

Fig. 8. 2

Source: For 1955-1985, Annual Report of Commissioner for SC/ST; 1993-1997, Commission for Scheduled Castes/Scheduled Tribes, Delhi.

Table 8.3: Household Type for Scheduled Caste and Others

Category	*Rural*											
	Self-Employed in Agriculture		*Self-Employed in Non-Agriculture*		*Agriculture Labour*		*Non-Agriculture Labour*		*Others*		*All*	
Year	87-88	93-94	87-88	93-94	87-88	93-94	87-88	93-94	87-88	93-94	87-88	93-94
Scheduled Caste	41.21	27.71	41.6	38.19	59.77	60.00	46.49	41.44	29.98	29.00	50.07	48.14
Others	27.68	25.57	31.42	29.49	53.30	52.34	34.45	35.59	19.26	20.51	34.37	31.29

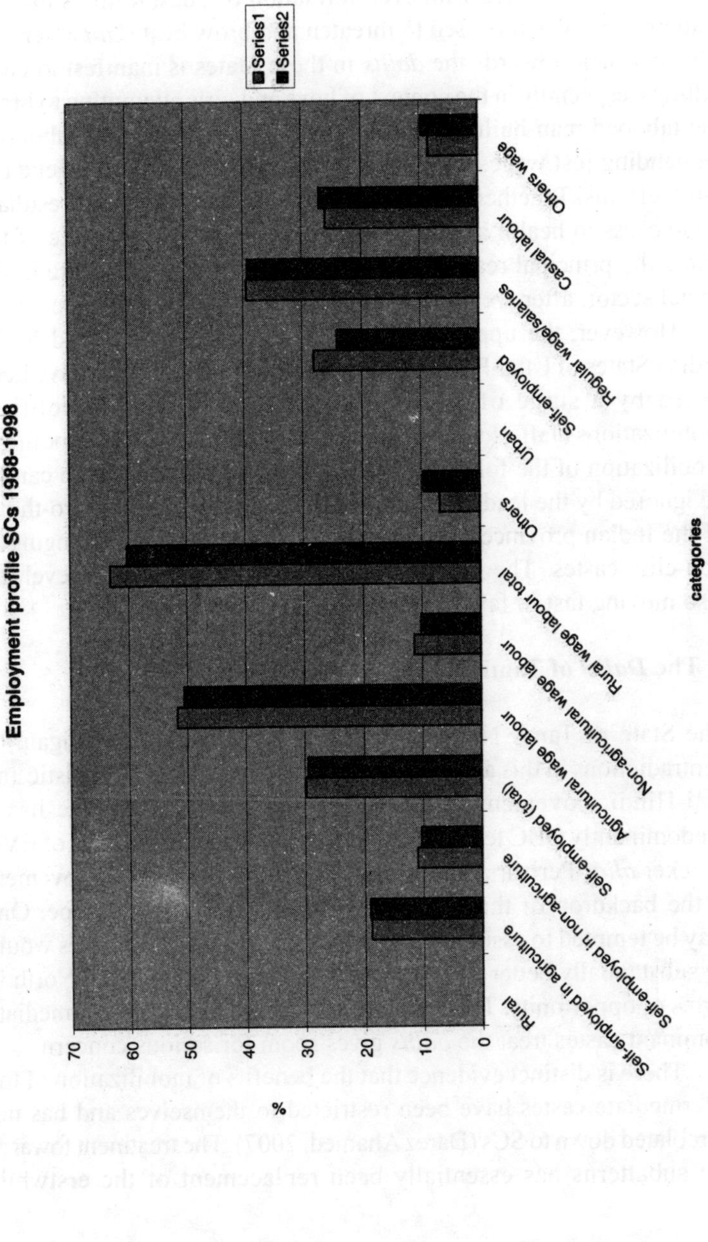
Employment profile SCs 1988-1998
Series1
Series2
%
70
60
50
40
30
20
10
0
Rural
Self-employed in agriculture
Self-employed in non-agriculture
Self-employed (total)
Agricultural wage labour
Non-agricultural wage labour
Rural wage labour total
Others
Urban
Self-employed
Regular wage/salaries
Casual labour
Others wage
categories

Fig. 8.3

approaches to weaker sections of society, the caste ridden North Indian States generally chose to ignore their genuine plight. The persecution of the serfs continued with even formation of quasi militias like the Ranbir Sena which is used to threaten and brow beat *dalit* assertion. The apartheid towards the *dalits* in these States is manifest in caste killings, especially in the context of boys and girls attempting to break the tabooed man-built caste barrier and hoping to marry, labourers demanding just wages and the near completely subverted agenda of land reforms. Together with these explicit shortcomings the resultant non-access to health and education facilities makes the State of the *dalits* the principal reason why India needs to do much more in the social sector, after six decades of self-determined development.

However, the upper caste elite of the above mentioned North Indian States of Uttar Pradesh, Bihar, Rajasthan and Orissa have been jolted by a surge of Backward/Scheduled Caste led political mobilizations (Jafferlot, 2003). Each State has a formidable political mobilization of the formerly weak sections of society which cannot be ignored by the leading political formations. More than two-thirds of the Indian provinces are now led by chief ministers belonging to non-elite castes. The political formations in the national level are also moving fast in favour of the OBC-SC formations.

3. The *Dalits* of Tamil Nadu

The State of Tamil Nadu (Fig. 8.4) is an interesting amalgam of contradictions in this aspect. Sporting a vibrant anti-brahministic and anti-Hindi movement in the fifties and sixties, the State has a predominantly OBC led political mobilization. The teachings of EVR Naicker *alias* Periyar and the Dravidian anti-caste Hindu movement is the backdrop of the highly dramatized political landscape. One may be tempted to assume that the lot of the Scheduled Castes would be substantially better than the caste ridden societies of the North in terms of opportunity. This test case of how the liberated intermediate dominant castes treat the *dalits* gives room for serious concern.

There is distinct evidence that the benefits of mobilization of the intermediate castes have been restricted to themselves and has not percolated down to SCs (Darez Ahamed, 2007). The treatment towards the subalterns has essentially been replacement of the erstwhile

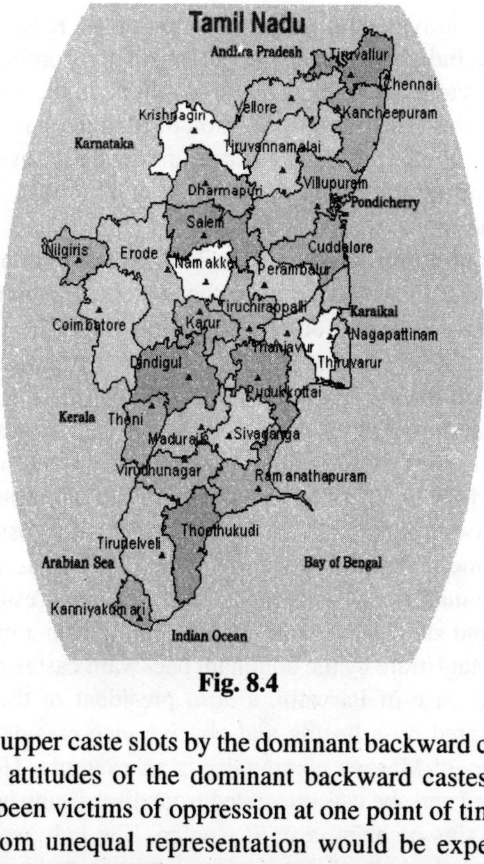

Fig. 8.4

suppressive upper caste slots by the dominant backward castes of the region. The attitudes of the dominant backward castes who have themselves been victims of oppression at one point of time, and still suffering from unequal representation would be expected to be different. But the field reports from Madurai, Tamil Nadu point to a State of transitory flux and tension.

Suppression and suppressive co-option of the emerging *dalit* leadership is reported afresh from nascent rural democratic institutions—the panchayats. Madurai district of Tamil Nadu has several reports of caste based parochial repression against SC communities. The district has 13 per cent SC population and the differential achievement in literacy rates is notable, with SC achievement at 60 per cent opposed to general achievement at 75 per cent. The first *dalit* graduate of the district was reportedly murdered by caste Hindus for daring to wear trousers and pass the upper caste area. Two graduate students of the Annamalai University who fell in love across caste barriers (the boy being an SC) were done to death by their own relatives. The *dalit* celebration of Mr. K.R. Narayanan's ascendancy to Indian Presidency (1998) resulted in torching of twenty *dalit* hutments and damaging a hundred others. In the Independence Day of 2003, the district administration of Madurai had to intervene to save a *dalit* President of a Panchayat from upper caste ire for his 'crime' of hoisting the national flag, which was in fact his constitutional privilege.

Analysis of crime against SCs in Tamil Nadu State and Madurai district (Table 8.1) would point to the sustained leadership of the district in State-wide data on crimes against SCs. The intermediate castes are commonly accused in most reported offences unlike the northern Indian States.

Blatant discriminatory practices like having separate drinking glasses in tea shops, disallowing ownership of land, refusing use of common land for burial of dead bodies, refusal of employment, are seen as backward dominant caste's responses to *dalit* assertion. Any challenge to the *status quo* is put down heavily. Even as late as 1996, the day light murder of Murugesan, a newly elected President of rural panchayat (and six others) as he was returning from a meeting with the District Magistrate by the dominant backward castes point to this. The recorded case of Parvathi, a *dalit* president of the Panchayat when confronted by a hostile and abusive vice-president from the locally dominant Marava community is an example. Her meetings were disrupted and she was prevented from discharging her functions for the twin sins of being a *dalit* woman. The lady was persistent enough to seek the help of district administration and resume duties. She won a re-election after even gaining the support of even high caste women largely due to the determination she showed.

Despite the churning, the elements of segregation and resistance operate in the State. The *dalit* dwellings (Cheris) are routinely located outside the village proper and away from common amenities. The *dalits* have *de jure* rights which civil authorities need to enforce on unwilling dominant groups with whom the SCs have to share resources and services.

4. Mobilization and Empowerment

The 1990s have seen active *dalit* mobilization and politicization across

Tamil Nadu. The media reports of pervasive discrimination brought regional action committees together and they initially faced severe resource crunch and lack of skilled leadership. The personal skills and media space which comes only at a cost in a market economy were also inadequate. Leadership gap was filled with the emergence of leaders like K. Krishnaswamy and Thirumavalavan. These inspiring leaders got dedicated full time *dalit* workers together and started mobilizing. Resources were forthcoming and the movement is well entrenched as of now, a force to reckon with, which no mainstream power brokering political entrepreneur can afford to neglect.

The biggest qualitative difference of the mobilization is the distinct element of identity the organized *Cheri* sports. Erecting the flag and emblem of the movement in a common public place marks this allegiance and proclaims the fact that the *Cheri* is not stand-alone. Its roots to the larger political spectrum of the State level *dalit* organization are also made known. Seclusion of the *dalit* voter from the allegiance to mainstream parties like the two factions of the DMK (Dravida Munnetra Kazhagam) [roughly: Dravidian advancement party] in protest of their treatment as cluster of votes was the first strike strategy of the *dalit* movement.

By 1996, Krishnaswamy's Dalit Panthers India entered electoral politics and won a seat to the provincial legislature. From 1999 *Dalit* panthers are contesting and influencing State politics. The *dalit* organizations are still nascent and have not generally shared power. They are influencing the policy process from the side rings. Upper caste response ranges from fully supportive to fully derisive. Some respondents told Darez that the *dalits* should accept their lot and not try to rise and 'rebel'. The response from the *dalit* movement—in the words of a young *dalit* woman activist would counter it thus: "Fighting the tyrannous upper castes and dying is better than this demeaning existence". Desperation is driving some of them to violence.

Violence has merited some adverse press and middle class aversion to *dalit* movement. Suddenly the society used to the hopeless groans of the *dalit* is hearing his war cry. His use of the decades old identity politics perfected by the hypocritical Indian upper caste intelligentsia against them is ironically significant. While the original radicalism of the Dravidian mainstream parties has whimpered down to compromises due to successive mal-governance, amongst others, the *dalit* movement offers avenues for pure democratic expression. In fact the chunk of the movement is dominating the civil society actors in the State. Therefore, the *dalit* movement in Tamil Nadu would be a case of the deepening democracy by creating new spaces and is a cultural revolution in itself.

The mobilization has also exposed fractures and fissures in the *dalit* situation, whereby some groups are allured by the intra-SC stratification. There are references to such differences as weakening the pace of the movement (Darez Ahamed, 2007). The *dalit* movement, therefore, is better viewed regionally as different levels of organization and cohesion. The presence, of more than seventy *dalit* organizations in Tamil Nadu would point to this fact. The largest are reported to be Dalit Panthers India (DPI) and Puthiya Tamizhagam (PT) [new Tamil Nadu]. There are strict specific caste bases to them, but seem to cooperate on mutually significant issues.

Darez Ahamed (2007) also raises the issue of whether caste based mobilization aiming at a casteless society would be a contradiction in it self? This question on methodology may be less relevant in the exigency of being collectedly relevant in a competitive democracy where votes determine—though imperfectly—access to immediate resources and even survival. That large democratic mainstream political organization would harbour *dalit* interest at its core is also suspected.

5. Exclusion in Madurai Panchayats

The present reports of caste based exclusion reveal a pattern in three villages in Madurai district of Tamil Nadu.: Keeripatti, Pappapatti and Nattaramangalam. The problem has been lingering on for the last few years after the new Tamil Nadu local self-government legislation which reserves certain village administration positions to the Scheduled Castes. The crux of the conflict is the opposition of the locally dominant though statutory backward Pramalai Kallars (Dumont, 1986) also known as Thevars to the implementation of the legislation and the various constitutional provisions enforcing SC representation.

The cooption of the Kallars has always been difficult. Fiercely independent and martial, successive feudal and colonial administrations have followed an approach of tact and appeasement towards them. There are records of Nayaks, the pre-independence rulers paying head tribute to them. Kallars have a recorded history of refusing to pay taxes to many dispensations and they did glorify violence. The name Kallar means thief in native Tamil. Many of these assertions may no longer be valid in the semi-urban milieu, but the detailed accounts of the experience in the three mentioned Panchayats point to some elements of the remaining aggressive past.

Table 8.4: The Strategy of Inclusion in Madurai

Strategy	*Keeripatti*	*Pappapatti*	*Nattaramangalam*
Key actors	DM, RDO, SI of Police, BDO CHELLAKANNU (CPM	DM, RDO, BDO, SI of Police, THANKARAJ (CPM), MANICKAM (VAO); SHGs	DM, RDO, BDO THANKARAJ (CPM)
The negotiation style of administration	Carrot and sticks Youth Centred	Divide and manage Mobilize SHGs	Creating alternate Leadership Forcing competition
Key animator	Murugan, selvam (Kallar youth)	Socrates, Krishnan, (Kallar youth) Chellakannu Thevar, Mayi noon meal organiser, local government servants	Muthuramalingam, Thevar (ex Army), Pandi (contractor)

The British colonial period saw the application of resource development as appeasement. The Kallars of Melur were offered water from the Periyar dam after assurances of good conduct and acceptance of nominal taxation. This is cited as a success of the works department over the law enforcers.

However, the Kallars of the Usilampatti area were difficult (Fig. 8.5). They were fiercely independent and were not able to come to a consensus on accepting British suzerainty. Therefore, frustration set in and the British administration notified them as criminal tribes.

Records indicate 38,000 criminal cases against Kallars making them the most prosecuted community in British India.

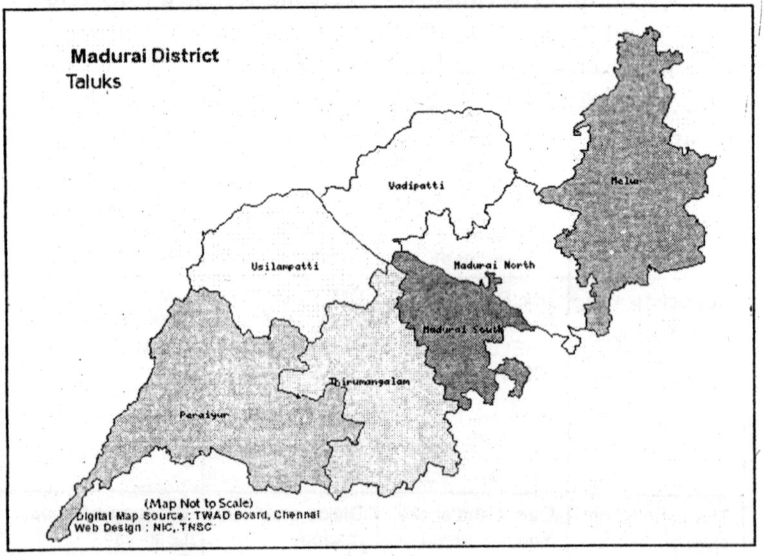

Fig. 8.5

Post-independence, the Kallars have relied on a hierarchical quasi- political organization to suit the needs of the new democratic institutions, namely the Pasupon Muthuramalinga Thevar led Forward Block. There is no marked ideology and no larger electoral presence in provincial or national legislatures. Some argue that the avoidance of mainstreaming is deliberate since the cost benefit of local dominance over resources is best suited by an endogenous organization. The Dravidian parties have also been lukewarm to large scale induction. The geography of the Usilampatti hills is also prohibitive of large scale interchange of ideas and knowledge.

The subconscious of the Pramalai Kallar's mind is still vivid with his native State organization. They consider that the Kallar area is divided into eight *nadus* (provinces) further divided into village aggregates called *oorus*. Each *ooru* is led by *ooru Thevar* and *nadu* by a *nadu Thevar*. Each *ooru* have separate martial tradition with their own folklore of legendary successes and sacrifices replete with their own mythological and magical realist imagery. The most sacred and revered temple of the Kallars is the Oochandamman temple situated in the Pappapatti *oor*. The problem of opposition to *dalit* leadership arose in these two villages only because Pappapatti-Keeripatti is the *thalainadu* (head village) and no other village in *thalainadu* is reserved for SC category. The Kallar areas have another division called the *upagramams* which are separate from *nadus*. (Nattarmangalam is an *upagramam*). The active celebration of the glorious past and rites of honour are common and the psychological landscape of the Pramalai Kallar reveals 'drenched in blood' relics of a basically tribal, domination led strategy of survival.

6. The Genesis of the Current Crisis

Post 73rd Amendment to the Constitution of India, making it mandatory for provincial governments to enact separate legislations and conduct elections every five years for local self-governments, Tamil Nadu State Government has enacted such local law. The law and its implementation do not reveal a radical shift in the development and resource allocation strategy of the State as can be seen in the neighbouring State of Kerala. There are reports that the entrenched forces at State level have low interest in promoting local self-governments as vibrant centres of civic activity. Unlike Kerala where the entire elections to LSGs is fought in party and coalition basis, the village Panchayats which form the lowest tier of the local self government in Tamil Nadu have personality or caste based elections.

The Tamil Nadu local law for the local self-government organizations provide for 33.3 per cent reservation of seats for women. For SCs and STs the seats are reserved in proportion of their respective local population. The census accounts are taken to be the basis of the same. The powers of deciding which seats are in the reserved category allowing contest only from the SC/ST community is between the State government and district administration led by the district magistrate (DM), who is usually an officer posted by State government but borne on the federal Indian Administrative Service (IAS) and hence expected to have an All India outlook. As in some other States this power of deciding the reserved seats is not delegated to an independent State Election Commission. The Tamil Nadu model could, in hindsight, be pernicious since the ruling formation at provincial level gets to decide which seats are to fall in the reserved category in a particular year.

The three specific villages in question have not objected the methodology of deeming their villages to be in reserved category village heads, but the right of the higher democratic formation to dictate their leadership across local custom. Though Nattaramangalam had allowed a *dalit* in the previous elections the mobilization in Pappapatti and Keeripatti soon reversed the tide and inhabitants belonging to Kallar community staunchly opposed the usurpation of the heredity dictated custom. This open denial was highlighted in the regional press.

7. Responses from State Level

The State level political formations chose to soft-pedal the issue since the Kallar caste is a dominant multi-constituency presence and they possibly wanted to weigh the *dalit* mobilization and test it for strength for electoral dividend before supporting their cause. The Dravida Munnettra Kazhagam (DMK) was initially lukewarm to the cause of the *dalit*s as was All India Dravida Munnettra Kazhagam (AIADMK) when they handled the State power. The only explicit support for the *dalit* cause came from the left parties which are not electorally decisive at State level. The *dalit* organizations got immense support from various civil society organizations and media. Despite the highlighting in the regional press the State Election Commission or State Government were unable to marshal a strategy of dialogue with the dissenters. The general approach at the State level was to leave the action to the district magistrate and adopt a 'wait and watch' approach.

The anticlimax came when the *dalit* organizations sponsored a *dalit* candidate to take on the local dominance and fight out the elections. It may be difficult to comprehend the inability to fight elections against the Kallars. The reasons are economic as most *dalit*s in the area are wage labourers in farms of Kallars. Besides this there is a long tradition of respectful obedience to the Kallar domination which in the absence of education or exposure to ideas of emancipation which has been reinforced by fears for the consequences if they chose to dare, as in Melevalau murders mentioned herein.

Academics suggested many solutions to political parties which were not enthusiastically received. One was to get the political parties to contest elections displacing the caste interest, the other was to stop the development grants to the area until the legal proviso are honoured as attempted in Madhya Pradesh in a case of traditional ritualistic live burning of a widow (*sati*). They were not prepared for any drastic pressure tactic which might antagonize the resourceful Kallars and not possibly yield a commensurate mobilization from the *dalits*.

The recent emergence of DMK to State power in 2006 with a majority of members of State legislatures from the Usilampatti tract formed the backdrop of the current efforts. Suddenly DMK found itself under pressure to deliver on the *dalit* question. The left parties, *dalit* organizations and civil society organizations backed the DMK to the legislative assembly election on these issues amongst others and it was pertinent that they deliver.

Various measures of hostility were being adopted by Kallars to stop the conversion of general category seats to reserved seats. We mentioned the Melevalavu incident where the first *dalit* president of a local panchayat, was hacked to death along with six others (1996). While the memory was still a festering wound in the minds of the *dalits*, the other oppressive measures included communal boycott of *dalits* by refusal of work, denying access to shops, temples, panchayat offices, noon meal schemes, community halls, public toilets or even walking near caste Hindu residential areas. This most repressive aspect of Hinduism, which compelled its lower leadership strata to abandon the religion as a whole and adopt Buddhism in 1937 was perpetrating its principal ideology of a stratified and secluded knowledge society where the fruits of development are to be restricted to a few at the cost of many, ironically through new democratic instruments.

Reports of shop owners who sold to *dalits* were being fined rupees one thousand ($30) by the community, SCs restricted to walking on the ridge of the roads so as not to come close to the dwellings on either side, refusal to use public amenities, preventing even private transport from halting near the Dalit hamlets, pelting stones at *dalit* hamlets in the nights, and disallowing any land purchase or ownership rights apart from the communal lands of government were documented as 'suffocating and smoking out tactics' unleashed by the Kallars.

8. The Strategy of the Administration

With limited clear mandate from the State administration, it fell upon the young District Magistrate (DM) of Madurai, an IAS officer of about ten years of experience to develop and implement a strategy of inclusive elections acceptable to both parties in the dispute.

His first actions were to streamline the administrative hierarchy of the Usilampatti tract and put his own house in order. The weeds in the system were identified and removed. They included officials known for their sympathy to the Kallar cause and also known to divert development funds by corrupt practices. He also set a personal style of direct engagement bypassing the village elders. He would meet the villagers in the respective hamlets including those of the Kallars. Meetings in the community halls were stopped since the Kallars were known to prevent the *dalit*s from attending or raising the issues.

For quite some time the discussions pertained only to development issues and the election issue was not mentioned at all. In the process the DM also identified various individuals who could be thought leaders of the various elections and established personal rapport with them. The idea was to use them as animators later. Similarly the key persons who were instrumental in the Kallar resistance were also marked out for later neutralization. Deterrent action was meted out to junior officials who were seen colluding with Kallar leadership. An atmosphere of non-favourability developed to Kallar's dominance ideology, eroding their edge in the society.

During the process of identifying and activating the crucial players in the stand off, the district magistrate and his team also sanctioned about Rs. 50 lakhs (100,000 US Dollars) worth of minor development works. Local leaders irrespective of caste formations took part in getting the works done. During such formal communications the DM reasoned with the leaders on the need to expand the welfare schemes to weaker sections. In the meantime the press was requested successfully not to highlight the caste conflict issue to provide for reflection and reconciliation time amongst the key players.

The district administration also identified the potential candidates who might be put forth in case elections were declared. Neutral civil society players and left parties opened dialogues with educated elements within the Kallar formation and found volunteers especially amongst government functionaries who, with the aid of the people did eventually conduct the elections.

The inclusion of the larger Pramalai Kallar grouping in the debate was key to ending the deadlock. In fact the opinion of the dominant community in perpetrating the caste based discrimination itself was the handiwork of a few. Mobilization of within Kallar opinion against the irrational imposition of casteist discrimination marginalized the hard-line dissenters. The reductionism in our narration obviously masks the thousands of negotiations the DM's team had to hold to bring in a level playing field.

The educative negotiations with the respective communities reached tipping point when the sizable section of Kallars started feeling primitive and defensive about their articulated stance. Police had to physically protect the candidates in the days up to the poll. DM held intensive development initiatives throughout to sway the attention from the divisive tensions of elections.

The left parties contested all seats including ward members on the district administrations suggestion to foist contest. This provoked the *dalit* formations to win all those seats. This was considered a great service to the idea of emancipation where by the left parties adopted tactical candidate positioning for a larger end. The number of contesting candidates also impacts the votes polled and thus the overall vibrancy of the electoral process. The left parties who supported the *dalit* cause did not reap rich benefits out of the elections. Though they were more successful in the ward-sabhas, the village panchayat seats were won by *dalit* members contesting as community. The successful conduct of elections culminated in a mass communication programme titled social equality function. All the facilitators of the *dalit* assertion were facilitated by the provincial Chief Minister in Chennai, the provincial capital. The three panchayats were given Rs. 20 lakhs (50,000 US Dollars) each as special development assistance.

The reasoning of the DM's strategy rose from the finding that the Pramalai Kallars were a highly individualistic group whose opinions were captivated by few individuals. Isolating the resistance to *dalit* participation to a few was crucial since the community had to be dissociated from it. Thus, the strategies to co-opt, assist and wean away the saner elements succeeded. Thus dividing the popular opinion within Kallars was the key to the breakthrough. Care was also taken to see that the posts of panchayat presidents do not fall vacant due to lack of participants. The ward members advise and control the elected presidents and they took office together.

Now we briefly consider the specific dynamics of the process described above in the three panchayats in question.

9. Nattaramangalam: Splinter Leader Forces Contest

In 1996, the first SC reservations took place here and election was effortless. Kallars did not object at all and an SC candidate won here as President. He was rated fairly successful in terms of welfare measures as well. In 2001, elections the reserved status was meant to continue, which meant that the Kallars could not regain lost ground, which they were hoping for. Pappapatti and Keeripatti erupted and Nattaramangalam joined them in the active resistance.

Nattaramangalam was special since most of the officers like Block development officers and police officers belonged to the Kallar community. Winning their confidence and getting them to act impartially was a Herculean task. The interplay of public service ethos and the way the omnipresent ethos of caste impact results in development and welfare is underlined here.

The service of Muthuramalingam, a discharged progressive army man belonging to Kallar community who was the opinion leader here was enlisted. He agreed to contest for a ward position and also garner support for an SC member who would contest for the president's position. When this was going on the Kallars also got into their mobilization and had talks with the SC community. The Kallar leadership did not want a neophyte to snatch their position as king makers and they fielded 'their own' candidates for the post of President from the SCs.

Thus the initiative of this splinter Kallar agent split the Kallar opinion in three ways and ensured an SC candidate supported by one of the groups to win the seat with majority so as to satisfy the electoral law. The logic behind supporting an SC for president was that the group which wins would get to be the vice president and can hope to control and influence the president's actions to a great extent. DM also assured that the rotation of reserved status would move on to other panchayats later.

Campaign was hectic and Kallars met the election propaganda expenses of the SCs as well. Severe contest resulted in winning by Ganeshan of SC (Pallar) caste by 132 votes. Muthuramalingam became vice president as nine others supported him.

Apart from the tactically divisive strategy the DM, he also announced numerous development schemes in key sectors like housing, community health and welfare facility, public transport, etc., which would be fulfilled on the conclusion of elections.

10. Keeripatti: Galvanizing Youth Power

Keeripatti election management was further complicated by the involvement of criminal gangs. The local Block Development Officer (BDO) thought of a youth mobilization strategy to overcome this menace. The lack of employment opportunities was considered to be the prime mover in the youth aberrations in Keeripatti. Uneducated youth of Keeripatti were doing smuggling of narcotics. Police Raids and recoveries are regular; a case of several kilograms of *ganja* (cannabis) seizure was reported weeks before the elections. Besides costly criminal court cases were on between Kallar and SC youths, adding to the frustration.

Compounding the issue was the widespread belief amongst Kallars that the SC victory will earn them the wrath of the Kallar martial deity 'Oochandamman'. Numerous examples on the wrath of the deity spread like wild fire. It was described that all former challengers to the Kallar domination earned the wrath of the deity and died or lost heavily in trade or agriculture. The Kallars had apparently pledged that the *dalit*s would be their serfs for ever, three hundred years ago before the deity.

The BDO was the front line tipping point leader in the exercise. He was asked to assure all developmental work in the Block. Former president Annakodi Thevar was asked to support the SC reserved elections. District Magistrate personally interacted with Keeripatti Panchayat for knowing their needs.

The youth mobilization turned the pressure against the latent conservatism. The district administration was actively encouraging filing of nominations. Six nominations were filed and Mr. Baluchamy (SC) was elected convincingly.

The educated unemployed youth functioned as a pressure group here. They were involved in the electoral process itself as facilitators. The officers had identified the youth who had a window to the world and who had an open mind about the issue in question. Precautions like allowing nomination filing to the distant revenue division office instead of the local block development office was done to monitor and control the process.

Development was another pitch where the district administration batted well. Rs. 60 lakhs worth of development works are taking place there as of now. Pooling of resources from the various developmental schemes has been done innovatively to meet the requirement.

A group which claims high involvement in grassroots democracy is the Kallar youth of the Panchayat. Once they shared a vision of inclusive development, they could surmount the baggage of the old guard.

11. Pappapatti: Self Help Groups as Animators

Pappapatti has a history of broken promises of irrigation schemes—the latest being the proposed Rs. 330 million 58th channel scheme which has not taken off since 1996. The construction of this is further entangled with the Mullai Periyar dispute with riparian Kerala and is not scheduled to start immediately.

Of the three villages in question this one had a reasonable calm between Kallars and SC communities. Temple also has common access for all communities. The mythology of Pappapatti would denote a sharing of the deities between Thevars and *dalit*s. The first 42 *Kula daivams* (family deities) were taken by the Thevars and last two were given to *dalit*s. The Oochandamman temple festival is attended by all communities including *dalit*s. The priest is from Kallar community. SCs are also honoured during the festival.

The crucial feature of the Pappapatti mobilization was the involvement of the self help groups. There were 44 such SHGs who generally lacked entrepreneurial skills. The lack of opportunity pointed to the lack of democratic space in the village to voice issues of development. The fallacy of stalling the legally mandated electoral process was made clear to the leaders by the members of the SHGs with the rational argument that the opportunity for Kallars would never come back if they were adamant to refuse *dalit* leadership.

They placed intense pressure on the local elders to accept the elections and better their future. Since administration was deferring development for want of elected leadership, they felt that the interests of youth would not be served if the stand off prevailed. The Revenue Divisional Officer of Usilampatti was instrumental in this mobilization. Youth mobilization through SHGs was the clincher in this case. Active use of the generation gap and the latent difference in perspectives to the issue of power sharing and tapping ambition to be financially self sufficient was crucial for success in Pappapatti.

In Pappapatti, post-2006 elections, the *dalit*s for the first time shared power with Kallars and decided on their future along with Kallar village elders in the sacred *Chavadi*—the centre stage of the village panchayat.

12. Discussion and Synthesis

Translating constitutional legalism into genuine empowerment is no mean task for democracies that suffered both colonial dereliction and native abdication in quick succession. It requires a vibrant media, purposeful public officials, political commitment and hard work with various civil society groups. Equitable splicing and imaginative embellishing and sharing of the development cake are critical in the exercise.

Public service has the twin responsibility of preserving and implementing the Constitution. But the policy process in India has not devised any rights or communication based strategy for enhancing this rationale. Therefore, even well meaning social legislation has to surmount opposition from convoluted, regressive logic in many States.

One implicit conflict is the lack of adequate political will from State level powers in solving organically important micro level issues as the Kallar-SC conflict narrated here. The trade off they perceive is not attractive enough for the political entrepreneur in aggregate. The ruling class at the State level—big governments—are obsessed with own priorities which are issues of definition. Problems of the marginalized do not figure in such high tables.

Therefore, the onus is on district administration and fringe groups to champion their cause along with media. In neighbouring Kerala also, analysis of the tribal land question would result in similar conclusions. After growing to a threshold, political organizations cross the sensitivity required for the 'worms eye view' and become 'birds of prey'—looking for the next onslaught on diminishing resources.

The efficacy, performance and future of the village panchayats are not examined in this summary. They are bold avenues of democratic empowerment which are drawing administration to come close to people's issues and address long pending issues such as caste discrimination. Without forcing contest in own citadel, the Kallar pride would not have accepted the *dalit* rising. The aggregate legislative assembly or parliament voting masks such micro level tensions of the polity which are akin to masked chronic coronary thrombosis, which needs early detection for sustainable cure.

The desirability of party based elections against individual or community based elections also needs to be examined. While the interest of State level parties may depend on the resource position of the panchayat, at least a few parties contesting seriously is a good option for ensuring mobilization.

The explosion of the majoritarian option—the strength in numbers favourable to women and *dalit*s is another solid possibility that local self-government offers. It obliterates the space of powerful vocal elite by mobilizing youth and informal community based organizations.

The district administration's tactic in drawing the Kallars at large into debating the desirability of the seclusion and linking it with their own uncertain future through youth agency and SHGs in addition to or along with activating locally influential leadership is the highlight in the entire episode.

It is also a sad pointer as how the *dalit* interest can be sabotaged in the absence of influential, energetic and reflective executive leadership in the districts. This calls for educative training for the future district officers and State officials apart from posing the question of this ultimate paradox in democratic development: Does grassroots democratization need micro management of the order we have described there, and if it so needs for a larger timeframe, can we be optimistic about its unattended future?

We are also hopeful for a better tomorrow for the descendants of Murugesan and others who were martyred since the caste consciousness is low in the succeeding younger generations. With the turn of another generation the oppressive caste bias in the Madurai district may be a thing of the past.

Commentators on the potential of the Panchayati Raj system in India have entered the realm of romantic delusions (Bandopadhyay,

2006) when they suggest the abolition of the office and institution of the district magistrate, portraying it as an impediment to the smooth functioning of the grassroots democracies. The field evidence reaffirms the faith of the depressed in the institution of the district administration as the only recourse representing law, helping them achieve representation. The perils of subjugating this constitutional office to parochial and pernicious distorted 'grassroots' visions cannot be an option.

The historic Poona Pact between 'the Father of the Indian Constitution', Bhim Rao Ambedkar and 'Father of the Nation', Mahatma Gandhi has the exclusive reserved constituencies for the SCs at its heart. In retrospect the concerns of assimilation which Gandhi and other leaders expressed and doubted strongly by Ambedkar as non-genuine seem to have empirical support after eighty years of operating electoral reservations as practiced. The SCs who suffer from disempowerment of various reasons have been in many cases unable to emerge beyond the great divide and force political participation. The assimilatory tactics have, by and large led to the bottom-line being the ability of *dalits* to seek support of various locally dominant and dominating backward and forward castes and garner resources, neither of which is possible in the short run without State apparatus decisively backing them. The high aspirations of the law makers in the local administration reform have generally been compromised in implementation without an equally mandated presence of purposeful State administration. The concerns of Ambedkar and Nehru when village self-government was debated as a vehicle of self-governance in the 1940s still resonate, raising new questions and demanding new answers.

Descriptions

BDO: Functionary of development department, administering block development.

Dalit: General, politically charged term the SC mobilizations use to describe their forced submissive status. Of late lower OBCs also prefer the term.

Ekalavya: Mythical low caste archer hero who was asked to give his archer's thumb as fee for the archery training he received from his Brahmin trainer sage "Dhrona" to preserve upper caste Arjun's supremacy. (From *Mahabharata*)

RDO: Revenue divisional officer, usually at rank of Deputy Collector, Administrator of Sub-district.

SI of Police: Sub Inspector/Station Officer of Police Station/ Out post.

VAO: Village Administrative Officer

Acknowledgements

We thank Mr. Rudhra Gangadharan, Director, LBSNAA and Mr. T. Udhayachandran, former District Magistrate, Madurai.

REFERENCES

Amita Baviskar (Ed.) (2003). "An Ode to an Engineer" in *Waterlines*, The Penguin Book of River Writings, Penguin Books.

Bandopadhyay (2006). Is the office of the District Magistrate still necessary? *Economic and Political Weekly*, November 25th, 2006.

Darez Ahamed (2007), Monthly dispatches and district administration assignment to LBSNAA.

Dumont (1978). A South Indian Sub Caste, Oxford.

Hugo Gorringe (2005), Untouchable Citizens: Dalit Movements and Democratization in Tamil Nadu, *Cultural Subordination and the Dalit Challenge*, New Delhi, Sage.

Jafferlot (2003). *Indian Silent Revolution*, Hurst.

Kheer (1954), *Dr. Ambedkar Life and Mission*, Popular Prakashan.

Pandian (2007). *Brahmin and Non-Brahmin: Genealogies of the Tamil Political Present*, Permanent Black Pub., 2007, xii.

Thorat (2007). On Economic Exclusion and Inclusive Policy, *The Little Magazine*, Vol. VI, issue 4 and 5.

Thorat (2002). Oppression and Denial, *Economic and Political Weekly*, Vol. 37, No. 6.

Viswanathan (2005). Dalits in Dravidian Land, *Frontline* reports on anti-Dalit violence in Tamil Nadu (1995-2004), Navayana Publishing, Pondicherry.

9

Operation Crisis Jet 101

A Simulation Exercise

B. Ashok

Prepared by:

Centre for Disaster Management
LBS National Academy of Administration
Mussoorie-248179, Uttarakhand.
http://www.lbsnaa.ernet.in/lbsnaa/research/cdm/index.htm

Preface

Welcome to Operation Crisis Jet 101. This Simulation exercise was developed by a course team the prestigious Joint Civil Military training course for officers of the rank of Joint Secretary/Brigadier equivalent and above. This course run by LBSNAA Mussoorie is meant to impart conceptual and operational clarity on security related issues facing the country.

The Simulations played for 4 hours (with a break of 20 minutes) calls for role preparations and strategic thinking in addition to thinking on one's feet and strong communication negotiation skills.

This general backgrounder is supplemented by confidential role specifications given only to the concerned participant and additional resources like maps, intelligence (dummy) briefs, etc.

I would like to mention the encouragement we received from Shri Rudhra Gangadharan and Shri Padamvir Singh, Director and Joint Director of LBSNAA respectively.

I received creative suggestions from Professors H.M. Mishra, A.S. Ramachandra and Deputy Director Shri Rajesh Arya. Without the strenuous efforts of Shri Indrajit Pal, Associate Professor in CDM, LBSNAA and Shri N.V. Joseph, Research Officer, CDM and the organizational skills of Shri Yogesh Giri and Sachin Agarwal in conducting the exercise, it would have been impossible to present it confidently. I also mention the prompt response from M/s Miditech Films in sharing the IC-814 film with us.

I do hope that this case exercise with the films and explanatory discussion will make the practitioner participants learn by doing, which is the best way to learn.

Yours Sincerely,
(Dr. B. Ashok)

Note for Participants

Please go through the enclosed material for a Role play. Kindly be conversant with the scenario for effectively playing your role in the exercise.

You do not have to imitate or act, only the strategy has to be copied for building an effective dynamic.

Note for Observer

Observe the players and report the key findings to the plenary at the end of role play. Focus on the decision making/information sourcing process than individual attributes. Please be brief and do give feedback without mentioning names or value attributes to a player's performance.

Introduction

1. This simulation is designed to be played as a game by four to five teams of participants (20 ideally) separated in as many rooms.
2. The game is divided into three phases (30 minutes each) with three fast developing scenarios with inputs reaching the teams by wireless (Synchronized VHF sets placed with each team) and written dynamic scenario inputs/feeds

including maps and intelligence feeds. Each team is also provided with some maps and logistical information from time to time.

3. Internet facility is also available with each team to verify/ research some pertinent issues they might need to refer. Inter-team interaction is permitted, during phase III, with permission from the game control. Any face to face negotiation will have to be with mutual permission and no force is to be applied in securing access to another team's room.
4. The emphasis is on developing alternate scenarios, debating the merits of progressed actions, understanding interests, negotiating the positions with each other, projecting future scenarios and testing their efficacy in a complex dynamic situation.
5. While the roles prescribed are simply guiding in nature, the options to innovate and invent should not be lost sight of. But one must always remember that the purpose is not to solve any issue dramatically but to understand the complexity of the dynamic situation and the various unexpected turns it can take while attempting a solution.

Background

Rockland is a large plural democracy surrounded by transitional States Brotherland, Highland and Eastland. The Northern latitudes of all countries are of high altitude (upto 7000 M) with inaccessibility. Partitioned in independence, by the erstwhile colonial power, the nations Rockland and Brotherland have fought three border wars over the disputed territory of Middleland which each claims is theirs. Rockland is fighting an externally supported insurgency which it has generally quashed with its powerful armed forces. Of late, the Middleland guerrillas have been attacking Army positions and engaging in bombings in a large scale. The counter terrorism agencies of Rockland have successfully captured several Middleland militants and Rockland claims that Brotherland intelligence is behind them.

Brotherland has never been a stable democracy and is currently led by a former General of Brotherland Army who usurped power from an elected Prime Minister who is in exile. After such usurpation hostile activities conducted under the General had led to a minor localized border war which went in Rockland's favour and was mediated to an end.

Rockland also shares a border with Highland which has seen fifty years of never ending civil war led by tribal factions. Though briefly under foreign control, the Highland government, recently formed by extremist elements calling themselves "Highland Brotherhood of Guerrillas (HBG)" has not yet been recognized by Government of ROR. No diplomatic relations exist between GOR and Guerrillas controlling Highland.

The other neighbour of Rockland, Eastland is in equally serious turmoil. Eastland was for most part of its independent existence under a suppressive Monarchy. The native nationalist Maoists have just come to power and its internal security system is only stabilizing after civil war. Eastland capital city is a favourite holiday destination and people from Rockland, Highland and Brotherland do visit there especially the new casinos which have come up. December is a Festive season for the casinos and holiday businesses.

Rockland and Brotherland have active sea access with standing Navies while Eastland and Highland are land locked. Rockland government is led by the Majoritarian Nationalist Party (MNP) which emphasize that Rockland is for Rockmen while Highland and Brotherland are mostly composed of "Brother Men"—both distinct religions and ways of life.

The reason for Brothermen to ask for a separate country some fifty years ago was that they did not want to be a minority in Rockland. Rockland's main opposition is the Freedom party which led its freedom struggle and claims to be non sectarian.

The Military capability of Rockland, Brotherland, Highland and Eastland are summarized in Table 9.1.

The Stakeholders for the Day

Team 1

National Crisis Management Team, Republic of Rockland (ROR)

This is the highest national crisis decision making body of the ROR. The ruling "Motherland party" of ROR has always followed the policy

Table 9.1

Asset	*Rockland*	*Brother-land*	*Highland*	*East-land*
Nuclear weapons	50	20	Nil	Nil
Missiles (Anti aircraft)	1000	500	40	10
Army (Units positioned in this sector)	400,000	100,000	2000 (Irregulars)	20,000
Airpower index (Based on Universal Units)	300	230	20	5
Naval Power Index	200	70	5	Nil
Commandos capable of storming Aircraft	15000	10000	100	50
Degree of Preparedness	70%	75%	90%	85%
Intelligence Strength	7/10	8/10	7/10	6/10

of promoting the majoritarian religious group's nationalistic tendencies. In fact its campaign to remove certain historic relics which were according to him insultingly constructed during a foreign invasion in the 14th century had paid it good electoral dividends in the general election held four years ago. Its Government is reaching its last year in power and is projecting the success story of ROR in the economic front as the 'Rockland shining' campaign across the country with a view to gain electoral dividends. The mood in the Motherland party is upbeat since the opposition is disunited and that its family led coalition does not have a strong plank against the 'development above all' plank, the Motherland party has successfully played. Plus the tough anti-terror laws Motherland Government had enacted against terrorism had succeeding in controlling the separatists in Middleland Province who were virulent and very violent in the last regime led by Freedom party.

Team Member (Overt Role)(5 Members)

[1] Prime Minister (PM)

Is a 70-year old freedom fighter-ideologue who is given to good living and poetry. Seriously suffering from arthritis has undergone double knee replacement in the last six months and is taking steroids. Suffers from medium obesity and talks haltingly. Though a brilliant orator and captivating parliamentarian, commanding great respect through six decades of selfless public service, prefers to delegate and forget. Suffers periodic memory loss and absent mindedness.

Depends heavily on key political advisors and bureaucrats, National security adviser and cabinet secretary.

[2] Home Minister

Healthy 66 years old mature rightist peppy politician, always quick for a catch phrase or sound bite, media darling, he is fighting fit and practice Yoga everyday. Grew up during partition, and relocated from Brotherland to Rockland during communal carnage. Identified to be more of a nationalistic hardliner, is a main motivator and strategist of the Motherland party.

Led highly successful mobilization of motherland party supporters in the last elections over the contentious historic relics issue and gained huge emotive support for the party. Not comfortable with bureaucracy, and an action oriented leader, he talks fast and takes fast decisions. It is known to all that there is intense discussion that given the health situation of the PM, the party is seriously considering him to lead it in the next elections due is less than one year. He has been very effective as HM and has delivered on counter-terrorism front. National police and intelligence under him have been very active in suppressing terrorist groups particularly in Middleland, and his success is being cited by his friends in the press as his strong credentials in the next elections.

Some human rights violations have been alleged against some key officers under him whom he has strongly defended.

[3] National Security Adviser

Sixty-five years old former career Foreign Service Officer who joined Motherland Party's Foreign Affairs group post-retirement, functioning also as Prime Minister's Key Political Secretary. Holding huge influence over the administration system and has a key role in important bureaucratic appointments including those of Cabinet Secretary, Key Ambassadors, etc. Soft spoken and halting external image is marred by occasional outbursts of violent temper.

He has never actually handled a hostage or calamity crisis calling for on the spot on-line decision making under uncertainty. His induction into high office post-retirement had caused jitters in the Cabinet Secretariat, since his proximity to the Prime Minister effectively transferred the seat of Power to Prime Minister's Office. He personally is a scholar and multi linguist in own right, well read and also a quick decision maker. Adheres to Motherland Party's Political Ideas and has frequently given lectures to their leadership study classes.

[4] Cabinet Secretary

Fifty-nine year old Career Civil Service Officer who has matured well and is not surprised at anything. He is likely to sit through an earthquake and wait for help. Always handled economic ministries where it was hard for most others to get anything from him. Excellent in carrying for favours and not annoying political bosses, he has a non-threatening demeanour and persona. Always smiling he chants choice Slokas from the Vedas and other Sanskrit verse suited for every occasion. Being deeply religious, helped his choice to a position in which he helped Motherland party's prospects very much. His hobby is Astrology and it is rumoured that his predictions, particularly for politicians is very accurate. It is not a secret that many important politicians on either side of the Parliament consult him. Decision making is his Achilles heel and he needs accurate and complete details for even the smallest decision to be taken.

[5] Chief of Intelligence Rockland

Career Police Officer who has been retained in the Rockland Intelligence Agency (RIA) for twenty years from the South. Fifty-seven years old sharp intelligence man, he has an action bias. His network and information's from Rockland's Key theatres are usually very accurate. He has been very successful in the present office which was given to him by the presenι PM overlooking six others under, support from NSA. However, he also thinks his inputs must go directly to PM, whereas it is the NSA who briefs and de-briefs him. He is little uncomfortable that his political reach is restricted, while NSA acts as buffer between him and the Cabinet.

Team 2
Border-City Local Authority (5 members)

[1] IGP (Mr. Reddy)

He is a veteran police officer with numerous commendations, Medals,

UN experience and extensive experience of Insurgency and extremist situation management. He has personally led an aircraft storming operation four years ago in the same bordercity. He has worked with the National Security Guard Commandos and has received Special training from Israel in using precision explosives to force open aircraft doors and storm them. An excellent team manager and leader he is selfless courageous and action oriented.

[2] DM (Mr. Kumar)

A young IAS officer of around 9 years seniority, this is his first high crisis call. He has successfully suppressed minor communal clashes etc. but has not experienced such a flash crisis. But he has composure, courage and tolerance and respects professional opinion. He is a fast learner and quick thinker too.

[3] SSP, Border City (Mr. Mahmood Hussain)

He is a rural boy who was bright in Math and succeeded in IPS after IIT. He has excellent managerial and technical skills but suffer from a little one-upmanship. He is senior to the DM by two years, therefore, he routinely send his Additional SP for his meetings. His professional skills are excellent but seniors; especially IGP Reddy has been some what critical of they call poor man management. He has reasons to ignore some of IGP Reddy's criticism, since he is an insider and considerably well connected politically.

[4] Director, Border City Airport (Mr. Pratham Singh)

Civil Aviation Professional from National Air Transport Authority of Rockland. He has 30 years of experience, at various levels, of airport and traffic management. All operational decisions on the airport are his, but he knows that as per national regulations he has to follow National Crisis Team's and local authorities' guidance in the matter. He is calm and composed and takes considered decisions only. He never loses his temper. He is deeply religious and planning to retire to an Ashram in the Himalayas. He has nowhere to go from here.

[5] Local Correspondent of 'National daily'

He is a 30-year old young reporter who has somehow sensed a scoop in the unusual build up of forces in Border city Airport. He knows

DM Mr. Kumar and generally favours him in reporting. He is trying to reach the DM and get some information on the administrations plans to avoid the crisis.

Team 3
Motherland's Negotiating Team (5 members)

[1] Chief Negotiator (Mr. Sarkar)

Career Foreign Service Officer, with substantial experience of Highland's Politics and Languages. Has been junior diplomat several years and knows many leaders. Has been out of touch for few years but is active in the Analysis desk. Excellent negotiator and calculates that Highland would value Rockland's political recognition of its Government as a very high diplomatic victory.

[2] Major General Bandookwalla

Previously Military Attaché of Rockland in Highland, he knows deeply about the insurgent's capabilities, etc. He can be Key contact/ leader for a military option and is entrusted with assessing the Potential for the same. Suspects civilian capability to deliver through negotiations and is keen to explore military action. Nevertheless respects authority and follows the negotiating team's commander's advice.

[3] Rodrigues, Intelligence Officer

Career intelligence officer who has been an active operative and analyst in Northland and Highland. Has excellent contacts and resources in the area. Speaks most Highland dialects and knows Highland tribal chiefs personally.

[4] Ambassador Kala (posted in Brotherland)

He has joined the negotiating team later and not happy about the RoR Govrenment's decision in sending in a much junior officer as Key negotiator. He thought he is most suited for the job but Mr. Sarkar's proximity to certain bigwigs was more influential this time around. Nevertheless he will act as a conduit for contacts with Middleland and contacting that Government through which he thinks he can influence the rebels in Highland. He is skeptical of any real positive outcome, but he is going to try his best.

[5] International Correspondent of Time: Mr. Roger

He is stationed in Crisis city, covering some political developments while the crisis has erupted. He is privy to the Highland Brotherhood's internal thought process and could be a valuable source. You are willing to be a go-between of Indian team of negotiators and Highland Brother leadership.

Exercise Players

Team 1: National Crisis Management Team (Rockland)	
Sl. No.	**Name of the Role**
1.	Prime Minister (PM)
2.	Home Minister
3.	National Security Adviser
4.	Cabinet Secretary
5.	Chief of Intelligence Rockland
Team 2: Border city Local Authority	
1.	IGP (Mr. Reddy)
2.	DM (Mr. Kumar)
3	SSP, Border City (Mr. Mahmood Hussain)
4.	Director, Border City Airport (Mr. Pratham Singh)
5.	Local Correspondent of 'National Daily'
Team 3: Motherland's Negotiating Team	
1.	Chief Negotiator (Mr. Sarkar)
2.	Major General Bandookwalla
3.	Rodrigues, Intelligence Officer
4.	Ambassador Kala
5.	International Correspondent of *Time* (Mr. Roger)

(Contd.)

Call Sign for VHF Wireless Communication		
	Team Name	**VHF Wireless Call Sign**
	Team 1	Echo Rockland
	Team 2	Echo Bordercity
	Team 3	Echo Motherland
Game Control Team		
	Name	**VHF Wireless Call Sign**
	Dr. B. Ashok	Alfa/Game Control
	Sh. Indrajit Pal	Charlie
	Sh. N.V. Joseph	Delta
	Sh. Sachin Agarwal	Echo Sachin
	Sh. Subodh Kumar	Echo Subodh
	Sh. Yogesh Giri	Echo Yogesh

Scenario I

Message 1: for the National Crisis team of Rockland from National Centre for aviation security:

Air Rockland Flight 101 from Eastland capital city airborne at 4.15 PM Local time has sounded air hijack transponder indicating a possible hijack/distress on board. Scheduled landing at Rockland capital city by 6.15 PM-alternates Nearcity A (Estimated flight arrival time 6.45 PM) and Bordercity (Estimated flight time 7.15 PM)

Action time for group: 3 mts.

Message 2: for the National Crisis team of Rockland from National Centre for aviation security:

Passengers on board 204, 79 Women and 25 children, VIPs for GOR: Only two Joint Secretary level officers,

ARF 101 passing 300 km North of Rockland capital city, possible destination: Border city or beyond from radar indications.

Estimated arrival 7.10 PM at border city……

Action time for group: 5 mts.

Message 3: From ATC Border city to National Crisis team

ARF 101 landed safely at 7.11 PM, Pilot informs that he is out of fuel… request refuelling for proceeding at the behest of the hijackers...destination unknown....request assistance and directions for action...Pilot indicates direct threat to hostages if refuelling is not done immediately.

Action time for group: 7 mts.

Message 4: National Crisis team to Local Authority of Border city:

See if you can stop the plane from flying out of Border city... We call for options for action... Explore options

Action time for local authority: 5 mts.

Message 5: Local Authority to NCT

Advise whether we can proceed with action to storm the aircraft... we have sixty commandos who have done the storming before and the same IGP is available...

Action time for NCT: 5 mts.

Message 6: NCT to LA:

See if you can shoot at the tires and can stop the craft from taking off...

Message 7: From ATC Border city to NCT:

Flight took off at 9.15 PM to westward direction possible destination Brotherland...

Action time for NCT: rest of first session.

Scenario II

Message 1: from Control to NCT:

Plane lands at City B of Brotherland, after an attempt at landing without lights, all safe... One few passengers are reportedly injured from stab wounds. City B airport is adamant that it will only refuel the craft and it must take off... Life of some passengers is in danger... Please advise...

Discussion time for group: 5 mts.

Message 2: Control to NCT:

Plane takes off to Highland... at 5.00 AM (Day II) possible destination crisis city... Estimated arrival time: 7.15 AM

Discussion time for group: 10 mts

Scenario III
Negotiation scenario:

Message 1: From Neg. Team to NCT:

WE know the demands of the hijackers: They are:

Release of three key terrorist in Middleland jails, jailed for murder. Working for separatist movements, retrieved body of terrorist B shot on escape from jail in Middleland and 200 million US $ for return of aircraft.

Discussion time 10 mts.

Message 2: from Neg.T to NCT:

Deadline set for 10 hrs for the release of the prisoners and handing over in crisis city... GOR has 10 hrs to decide its course of action......

***

Covert role (Only for the Player)
[Please do not share with others]

Team-1
Prime Minister (PM)

You dislike the Home Minister for his attempts to discuss the Prime Minister's deteriorating health in party fora. You think the HM is in a process of winning the party nomination for leading it in the next elections. Though the political advisers are showing confidence in you, there is every chance that in the next elections the party may choose to change the leadership.

You would be more comfortable with your key political adviser succeeding you for several interests. But he is far too junior to the HM, although he could have a better chance if the HM suddenly falls from grace or is seen to be inept in the popular media or party fora.

You are also fully aware that your efforts at normalizing the relations between Rockland and Brotherland have only succeeded partially. The military leadership of Brotherland has snubbed the past initiatives you took with a clear view of gaining a lasting legacy are under threat. After the spate of border hostilities in Rockland's border with Brotherland, you are also under pressure from your party hardliners led by HM who are pressing for cross-border hot pursuit of terror agents from Brotherland. You are also being criticized for being indecisive and too dependent on professional advisers.

It is a touch and go situation for you, you trust the National Security Adviser and the Cabinet Secretary who are your confidants, but deeply suspicious of the Home Minister and Defence Minister (who is incidentally from a coalition party).

Covert role (Only for the Player)
[Please do not share with others]

Team-1
Home Minister (HM)

Though you are deeply respectful of the PM's achievements, it bothers you that he is no longer fully mentally fit and physically able. You know that you are the party's natural choice for successor but you never know. You know that the party bigwigs may finally prefer a pliant government CEO whom you are certainly not.

You are nevertheless level headed and will not be mean to anyone. You are a patriot of the highest order and will keep national interest above all. It is another matter that for you national interest is majority interest of Rockland.

Covert role (Only for the Player)
[Please do not share with others]

Team-1
National Security Adviser (NSA)

Knows fully well that PMs is personally at his weakest position despite sufficient Economic Success. You are not very appreciative about PM's Key Political Adviser (KPA) whose meteoric rise in the PMO and party is putting your voice at a second decibel level. You have information about KPA's many omissions, commission and ingenuous strategies, but know PM's political future including constituency and relations with industrial houses are being managed by KPA. Success of KPA may not be in your interest in the short term. You are being kept at an arms length by the HM since you are very proximate to the PM and had to get PM to overrule HM and agree to a couple of sensitive appointments in the Home Ministry including that of National Chief of Intelligence of Rockland.

You are ambivalent as far as your future is concerned. It is more likely that HM will succeed the PM in the event of his stepping down before next selections. You know that HM's rise is good for the party and Government. but you are not sure of his continued support for your position. The Intelligence chief (COI) has been cozying up fast to the HM, despite your role in appointing him and is looking for a post retirement opportunity. A couple of newspaper editcrials have attacked your competence and it is known to you that both writers had shadow sources in the Intelligence agency.

Covert Role (Only for the Player)
[Please do not share with others]

Team-1
Cabinet Secretary

You know that the KPA's future is not bright from your own astrological calculations. He has a short life line. So you are taking care to not to invest too much on him. You have secretly predicted to the HM that he will be in PM's chair in three years. Even if Motherland party loses next elections under HM, his goodwill, will always be with you. He might offer a constitutional high officio, when you retire in four months and you might even be the civilian head of PMO under HM.

Covert Role (Only for the Player)
[Please do not share with others]

Team-1
Chief of Intelligence Rockland

You have respects but also professional rivalry with NSA and Cabinet Secretary. You do not regard Cabinet Secretary to be very professional, though formally reporting to him. NSA is dominating even key appointments in your establishment. Your proposals to post professional officers to key postings in Brotherland and also field operatives in Highland were overturned and virtually influential officers posted.

You doubt the competency of some of them he suspect that some are reporting directly to NSA sometimes giving updates first to him, later to you. You have an excellent understanding and relationship with the HM and hopeful that he succeeds the leadership battle. But you are also a confidant of the KPA and engaged in political tips for both. You are confused as to where to shift balance, once the succession race is on. You are also in touch with leader of opposition of 'Freedom Party' and have not closed your options.

Covert Role (Only for the Player)
[Please do not share with others]

Team-2
Border-City Local Authority IGP Mr. Reddy

You have been transferred, on your own request and are awaiting arrival of relieving officer, for over two weeks on account of illness of his wife.

Covert role (Only for the Player)
[Please do not share with others]

Team-2
DM Mr. Kumar

You are a little adamant once you take a position. Your seniors are reminding you that you need little more flexibility while dealing with local politicians. They think you suffer from a PR deficit though your development work is first class.

Covert Role (Only for the Player)
[Please do not share with others]

Team-2
SSP, Border City Mr. Mahmood Hussain

You are looking to prove professional excellence and pick up a posting in UN or Interpol. You are daring and led raids several against operatives of the Northland separatists with success. You are a good marksman and horse rider. Pulling off a daring rescue could bring you the limelight which could make the difference between policing petty theft and murder for another ten years or sitting across the Hudson river Offices drawing a dollar salary and pension.

Covert Role (Only for the Player)
[Please do not share with others]

Team-2
Mr. Pratham Singh, Director of Border City Airport

You have never understood why such junior people are placed in high office like DM's and SP's. You have had poor behaviour from some in this career and dislike the authority these people yield. You think they lack maturity and judgment at their young age. However you are willing to play by the rules, if you do not have to take huge risk.

Covert Role (Only for the Player)
[Please do not share with others]

Team-3
Rodrigues, Intelligence Officer

These operations have the potential to give you a most successful career in your hierarchy. As a professional operative you are thrilled of your involvement.

10

Innovations in Coastal Rural Water Supply

B. Ashok

There are about 10,000 water quality affected villages along the long Indian coastline. The main water quality problem making shallow surface sources non-potable is the excess Total Dissolved Solids (TDS) present. This, rising from saline intrusion from the sea or backwaters and the land development patterns causing accumulation of salts of sodium, iron, nitrates and clay poses serious threats for the drinking water availability of the coastal population. The seafaring majority of the coastal population is usually at a disadvantage from poor water supply and sanitation infrastructure. Lack of health amenities, illiteracy and lack of information compounds the crisis. The coastal areas account for most of the dismal national statistics in health indicators. One clear paradox is the high rate of economic activity and transactional ability of the coastline with access to modern communication and entertainment facilities contrasted to the dismal indicators in basic services.

Kerala Coast

Kadalundi Panchayat is a coastal village falling in the political district of Calicut (Kozhikode) in Kerala State. Table 10.1 would indicate the key data of the Panchayat and Fig. 10.1 will give the geography. Kadalundi is a typical coastal GP surrounded on all three sides by saline waters. In most wards the shortage of drinking water is acute and the State Government has been establishing a rural water supply project (*Jalanidhi*) supported by the World Bank which partly caters to the demand.

Fig. 10.1: Points of the Project in Kadalundi and Kodungalloore, Kerala

PLANET Kerala (PK), an NGO associated with the project was keen to explore further, the technical issues involving water quality in the coastal areas and has done some noteworthy work in the GP. The features of the PLANET technologies (which won a World Bank India Development Marketplace innovation prize in 2004) are their relative simplicity, low resource intensiveness, adaptability and effectiveness.

Neutralizing High TDS and making Water Potable

One of the earlier concerns PLANET Kerala was called upon to solve was the high number of domestic/community shallow wells falling to disuse following high TDS content. The TDS content surfaced usually in peak summer when the wells were at maximum use. PK could enumerate about 200 such wells in adjoining wards of the GP

Table 10.1: Basic Data on Kadalundi

District—Kezhikeds Panchagat: Kadalundi

Sl. No.	District	Kozhikode
1.	Total Area (in sq. km)	11.83
2.	No. of Wards	18
3.	Total No. of Households	6594
4.	No. of BPL Households	2548
5.	% of BPL Households	38.64%
6.	No. of SC Households	535
7.	% of SC Households	8.11%
8.	No. of ST Households	—
9.	% of ST Households	0.00%
10.	Total Population	36880
11.	Literate Population	32626
12.	% of Literate Population	88.47%
13.	No. of Women	18199
14.	% of Women	49.35%
15.	Details of Schools	—
	Total	20
	Private (Aided and Unaided)	16
	Government.	4
	Any Other	—
16.	Total number of students	9081
	KWA SCHEMES	
1.	No. of schemes in the GP	5
2.	No. of schemes functioning now	4
3.	Total number of households covered by the scheme	1446
4.	Households covered by functional schemes	1146
5.	Total number of private connection	434
6.	Total number of public standposts	143
	GP SCHEMES	
1.	No. of schemes in the GP	11
2.	No. of schemes functioning now	7
3.	Total number of households covered by the scheme	2405
4.	Households covered by functional schemes	1782
5.	Total number of private connection	268
6.	Total number of public standposts	147
	OTHER SCHEMES	
1.	No. of schemes in the GP	
2.	No. of schemes functioning now	
3.	Total number of households covered by the scheme	
4.	Households covered by functional schemes	
5.	Total number of private connection	
6.	Total number of public standposts	
	SANITATION STATUS	
1.	Number of households having toilet	6010
2.	Percentage of latrine coverage	91.14%
3.	Sanitary latrines	810
4.	Unsanitary latrines	5200
5.	Percentage of sanitary latrines over total latrines	13.48%

which were disused after the TDS figure crossed values like 5,000 parts per million (ppm).

Apart from salinity intrusion the most common other contaminants were identified to be salts of iron, nitrates and chlorides. Clay was also a frequent turbidity inducing agent that made consumption of the water impossible. PLANET had to consider lasting, simple and adaptable solutions to ignite villager's interest in their project.

Fig. 10.2: In this typical use of Backwashing, a cement gutter is created in the tiled roofing with PVC piping to lead the precipitation down.

PKs technical personnel tinkered with a very common and documented success strategy to neutralize the dissolved solids. The idea which they have subsequently called "Backwashing" is to use the roof top rain water harvesting to dilute the impurity and create volumetric surge of freshwater in and around the ground water area of influence of the well in question. PK technocrats knew from their hydrology that a well which has 3,000 litres or so as dead storage of excess TDS water if charged with precipitation of a few lakh litres of pure water from the rain would have a cleansing and diluting effect plus charging of the freshwater lens feeding the well. Visits to various households who have adopted the roof top backwashing technique revealed positive results with TDS going down to double digit values and water becoming potable again.

Fig. 10.3: Another variant of the innovation is to use UV resistant plastic sheet (Silpaulin brand) for thatched roofs.

The water not less than 1-3 lakhs litres for typical roof sizes in the GP, [25-50 square metres], goes down the ducts to recharge the well water. The recharge which is available for about 100-120 days in the average Kerala monsoon (3,200 mm rainfall) is seen to purify the water to the extent of TDS values as low as 56 ppm. The water level temporarily rises in the recharge fitted wells and pushes the freshwater lens wider. In addi ˙on to that, even the adjoining wells showed better quality due to the interference phenomena. There is further evidence to show that the gush of roof water also pushes the dissolved impurities into the adjoining soil profile. Studies of soil profile post- and pre-treatment show that the impurities have become stacked into the soil and formed bindings than stay in the water. Salinity, TDS profiles of the soil are increasing with the increase in the recharge rates. The observations would establish that the quantity matters in quality of well water, below a certain threshold of water pressure and surface tension, the leachable impurities tend to flow from soil to water and when the pressure in freshwater increases, the soil regains its possession. The main determinants of contamination were soil type, adjoining land use and freshwater content.

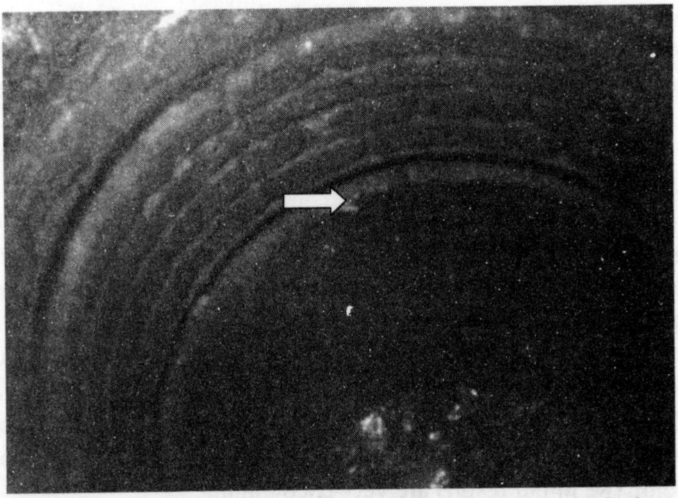

Fig. 10.4: It shows the TDS increasing contaminant—iron salts here—in the first well ring as attached deposits since the quantity has exceeded the dissolved levels.

The impacts of backwashing as a successful low cost strategy to tide over the quality problem in summer months when every freshwater source is stressed is obvious. The costs of water harvesting from a typical 50 sq. metre roof demands Rs. 1,000-1,500 depending on the quality of the connector pipes used. If the well yields one lakh litres during the summer post-treatment the cost of innovation per household is as low as Rs. 0.1 per litre of water obtained.

The success of the domestic stand alone recharging structures brought PK to its next logical question. Could the same principle can be adopted at a larger scale, i.e. to influence the freshwater lens of the entire village which is at threat from the sea water intrusion? Here they had to look for a natural agent which will do the function of protecting freshwater lens. The obvious candidates were plant biodiversity. Most contaminants found in the soil are nutrients to host of plants. Then the question comes, whether these plants cannot be used for absorbing contaminants from soil. The existence of scared groves in coastal areas along with large freshwater reserves is a common feature in these areas. Using community knowledge, a set of plants were selected—a mix of deep rooted and shallow rooted, as nutrient absorption from various depths. The plants include a mix of aquatic, semi-aquatic, terrestrial shrubs, trees and mangroves. Commonly used plants include—Mango (*Mangifera indica*), Circum (*Garcinia gummgutta), Thespesia populnea, Pandanus spp., Calophyllum inophyllum.* The mangroves, species identified include *Rhizophora mucronata, Rhizophora apiculata, Bruguiera spp., Avicennia officinalis* and *Acanthus ilicifolious.*

These species were experimentally proved to be excellent absorbers of excess nitrates, phosphates, chlorides and other chelates. PK is experimenting the plant based remediation (phytoremediation) with planting of saline absorbing tree belts across in two Tsunami hit estuarine islands—Sattar Island, and V.P. Thuruth near Kodungalloor (District Thrissur, Kerala). A mix of mangrove and coastal trees are being tried. Mangroves are planted here for arresting saline water intrusion, protecting the side slopes from eroding and to act as a bio-shield. The initial results are very encouraging.

As part of tsunami rehabilitation programme the Government. of Kerala had also made bold Statements about phyto-protection of susceptible coasts, but the remediation in practice has degraded into building rock barriers. It is universal experience that the sea wall strategy is a failure for sustainable sea protection. In UK for instance the managed realignment concepts have redefined the paradigm with sea being allowed access into agricultural land in between. It is the saline/freshwater interface that gives rise to typical mangrove species with their branching and robust root system performs the double functions of filtering TDS component as well as act as a diffuse barrier for coastal calamities like Tsunamis.

In Kadalundi there is a forest timber estate which offers excellent and copious amounts of potable water in all the wells surrounding that. The abundance of adapted salt absorbing species is the one performing this magic trick. Typical Avicennia patches seen all around the area show definite proof for its salt absorbing activity. The coastline has abundance of Avicennia leaves with glittering silvery extruded salt sticking prominently on them. (Fig. 10.5) Scale plantations of such salt nutrient conserving species—which

Fig. 10.5: Avicennia Overgrowth in Kadalundi Coast

PK calls phytoremediation—is another success story waiting to be scaled up. The cost implications (roughly one thousandth of the rocky sea walls programme) and early results are quite tempting for a scale application and long-term observations.

The third significant study result of PK is the efficacy of very shallow ponds structures in providing year round freshwater supply.

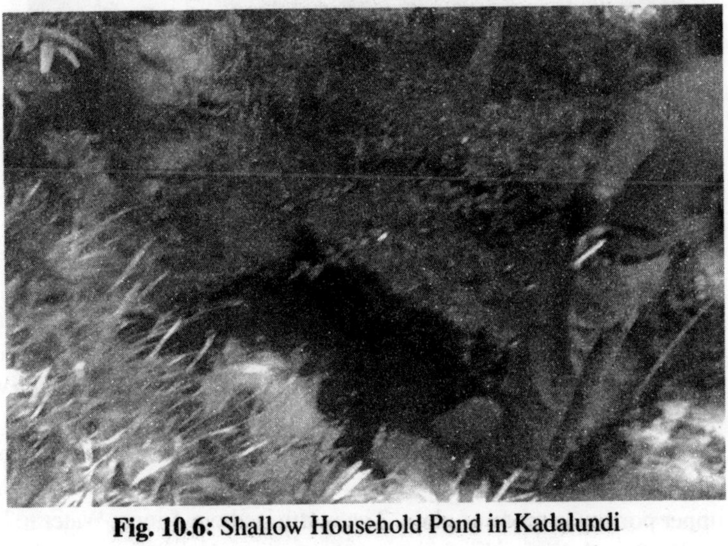

Fig. 10.6: Shallow Household Pond in Kadalundi

It may surprise many that Fig. 10.6 is an almost perennial source of drinking water for a family of four in Kadalundi. It is a four feet deep pond cut and laterite deployed all around in three layers. Protective plants are placed on all sides. The pond never dries up and the water is safe but for bacteriological contamination, solved by using boiled water. The point to note is that in the same spot well water turns saline in summer while the ponds which are tapping the upper freshwater lens remains fresh. This explains the practice of maintaining shallow ponds say 50 years ago, but was discontinued after the new technology shifted towards deeper wells and tap water. In Kadalundi we could come across a hundred-year old shallow pond which never dries up or water quality lowers even in peak summer.

Fig. 10.7: A Perennial Shallow pond in Kadalundi

Planet researchers also noted that there is huge demand for a cheap household desalination process that can be adopted by coastal households and institutions in the summer months when the freshwater squeeze is a reality. The result is a sleek and 100 per cent effective desalination unit using the sunlight as its energy source.

The structure and concept are again simple and cheap. Sand and clay mix is embedded between two aluminum frames of which the upper portion is made of glass. The width is about 1 inch. Water to be purified is fed into the frame at the top portion through ordinary

Fig. 10.8: Solar Distillation/Desalination Unit developed by Planet Kerala

plumbing pipes. The water trickles down through the sand and clay mix which gets evaporated due to the sunlight energy. This condenses over the comparatively colder glass and the condensate is collected at the lower edge of the frame and taken down by a duct and into drinking water bottles. The angle of incidence is kept at 25° where maximum effectiveness is observed and the results show water at distilled water quality 3 ppm TDS. The condensation rate is 2.5-3.5 litres per day, assuming six hours of good sun and three sills will give 7-9 litres of world class drinking water with no bacterial contamination.

Tests conducted by Department. of Gastrointestinal Sciences at Christian Medical College, Vellore, verifies that even with a bacterial load of 10^8 the output water is free of any trace. Seawater at 35 ppt (35000ppm) at the inlet has been reduced to 1-3 ppm TDS level thus performing effective condensation with practically no energy costs. The still cost Rs. 1,000 for each and provide a drinking water purifying solution which works for 200 days in Kadalundi conditions. The good point about monsoon days are that you are having adequate freshwater, from roof harvesting in any case. Prospective savings on the boiling costs in terms of energy for 200 days will justify the adoption of the innovation. Right now the PK personnel are collaborating with

LRAMP (www.lramp.org) a multi-lateral innovation development programme at IIT Chennai to develop marketable solar desalination systems which can serve the needs of the vast coastal tracks of India. This low cost household level potable drinking water system altogether treats physical, chemical and biological contaminations without a cost.

A variant of phytoremediation which PK has experimented for households use is worth mentioning.

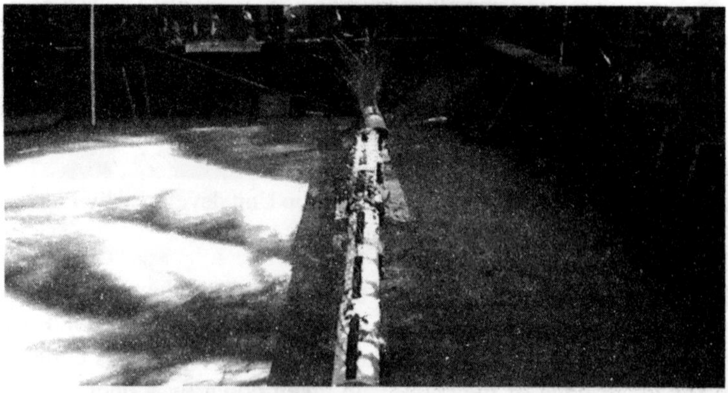

Fig. 10.9: Salinity Reducing Plants Planted in the Filtering Pipe

Figure 10.9 shows a longer larger diameter split duct into which the intake impure water is taken in. The sand layering within the tube is planted with Vetiver *(Vertivaria Sesmoida)*, Brahmi *(Bacopa monera)* and Tulsi *(Ocimum sanctum)* plants. The observations by PK as a result of the nutrient absorption by the active roots of these plants and the filtering action of the soil are testimony to reduced salinity and other dissolved and biological contaminants. All the chosen plants have higher nutrient removing and antibacterial properties. Experiments are on to determine the optimum time of retention hence the diameter, etc. of various piping. This is planned for recycling household waste water.

PLANET Kerala views the drinking water stress in any area a sign of extreme ecological stress. It observes that the non-industrial common pollutants like domestic garbage are made non-issues in the present debates (in Kadalundi GP there are no major water mining or polluting industries of significance). The results of the experimentations are disseminated through inventive IEC material and there is already great interest among the elected local representatives of Calicut. They would view that technology should be contextual and appropriate.

Explicitly, when communities realize that biodiversity is having a pertinent role towards maintaining water services and contributing towards their livelihood, a change in attitude, knowledge and skills is witnessed towards conserving/restoring ecosystem services. PLANET Kerala has been instrumental in facilitating these societal learning process through local experimentations, which concurrently increased awareness and practical results. Eventually, these processes helped to regain the communities lost right, access and control over the local ecosystem services.

Demystification of the technology through participation is seen to result in empowerment and lasting changes. Every homestead has to be its own watershed also to solve the coastal drinking water problem.

For visual documentation http://www.planetkerala.org/actions.htm

Further reading web links

1. Regenerating Freshwater http://www.planetkerala.org/downloads/RegeneratingHomesteadWaterSystems.pdf
2. Solar Desalination http://www.planetkerala.org/downloads/SolarDistillation.pdf
3. Backwashing http://www.planetkerala.org/downloads/Backwashing English.pdf

TEACHING NOTE NO. 1

(3. Crime Punishment and Redemption)

Time: 2 hours
Sub-groups: Prosecution and Defence.

Methodology

A plenary introduction to facts in case may be followed by dividing the 30 members group to five-six member groups who will debate whether the judgment of the High Court in the matter is in order or not. Three participants can play prosecution and the others defence in the sub-group. They can argue for 30 minutes, all the salient issues involved and return to plenary. In plenary selected spoke persons can present the strongest arguments for and against the discharge offered to the convict. In the second half the facilitator can play the most exciting issues and crime insights. The last 20 minutes can be in question-answer mode to further expand the argument.

Note

This case asks the crucial question whether our criminal justice system is essentially reformative or retributive. Society does not place much faith in the fairness of both judicial process and the reformative potential of jails etc. Therefore the net faith in 'redeemed' criminals is non-existent in society. Beyond the desirability of a convict contract joining a premier executive service of Government of India, the issue must be expanded to examine whether extreme retribution to a youngster's crime is desirable. Is there not a scope of rehabilitating a young aberrant in our society? Don't our systems have space for reform?

The success of the facilitator lies in guiding the discussion by arguing the convicts case, since most respondents are likely to take high moral positions intended to safeguard the value system of public services. The safeguards members of the service enjoy when accused under a crime of passion must be touched upon here. The fact that the High Court itself doubted the strength of proof against the convict can be emphasized. That the convict has spent five and a half years of his young life in prison may be pointed out. Whether it is desirable to imprison him further or is it more desirable to get his productive work under suspended sentence if he is genuinely repentant case be raised. What is the final test of a sound legal system? Is punishment the sole end of system? Does not repentance and desire to make good an individual's deficit account with society playing a role? Meditative justice systems being tried out in many countries like Norway can be cited. The facilitator needs to brush up his familiarity with the prosecution, sentencing and appeal procedure prescribed in Criminal Procedure Code and the Constitutional binders governing it. Sound understanding of appellate procedure is a must in doing justice to this case study.

TEACHING NOTE NO. 2

(4. Gas Trouble)

Time: 1 Hour

Methodology

Summary of case and diversion of class into 2 groups LPG users and dealers. Points can be taken at random to define their perspectives and then the salient features of the process involved in the administration's efforts to give effect to a basic consumer protection law can be highlighted. The distortions involved when special interest groups influence decision makers and play law with consumer interest can be examined. The learning points which the author has provided can be left as provisions for guiding executive action in such circumstances.

Learning Points

1. Despite odds, there are things which could be done.
2. Homework and research is painstaking but definitely rewarding. Once certain documents are 'there', or when rules/law is quoted, nobody can argue with that or deny the facts.
3. Doggedly following up matters of importance is vital. It should also been made clear to the public that we will indeed follow up and ensure results. This builds confidence in the public.
4. Do not expect everything to go in your way; there is no point in expecting an easy win.
5. I had a security of tenure and some shield of protection. I (The Assistant Collector) was the only person in the District assured of one year stint ! This may not always be the case. So be prepared to leave things mid-way and not feel bad. The real threat of my boss being transferred out loomed large but it was the least of his concerns during this issue.

6. While sending a report or submitting a line of argument, do not base your arguments on just one point, buttress it from all sides because you never know whether you get a second chance. Put the maximum justification on paper.
7. Never let others to guess your next move in a delicate situation. The best way is to avoid the possibility of a next move, i.e. as far as possible make it a one-move job. All the collected evidence/researched data can be fired at one go, and never in instalments. And all should be clearly made on paper so that the person who chooses to overrule it does so at his peril.
8. There are things that could be done. There are things that cannot be done. We officers are often not wise enough to distinguish between them. Political decisions are beyond our control and there is no necessity to try and control it either. Our work is to be done at our level, leaving the court open for other players who need to be acknowledged; we just need to record our position, especially on paper so as to influence other players and leave it at that.
9. The ending may not always be very 'feel good'.

TEACHING NOTE NO. 4

(5. Police Firing in Nasarathpur)

The case study can be circulated in advance (3 days) to the trainees who may be asked to think about their response, particularly with regard to the following issues:

1. The immediate steps which need to be taken once the report of death of a beggar allegedly due to assault by policemen is reported.
2. Why did the situation develop, as it did, on the first day?
3. Why did the situation aggravate on the second day? What should have been done to prevent firing on the second day?
4. If you were the SP, how would you deal with directions of the DIG?
5. If you were the DM, how would you handle the mob at the Collectorate on 13 October?

TEACHING NOTE NO. 5

(6. Tackling Commercial Encroachment)

Time: 1 Hour

This is a straight forward 'process' case which highlights the legal awareness and scheming called for from a young officer while taking on illegal alienation of Government land acquired for industrial purpose. Researching and understanding the difficult to get records and building government's the case without loopholes in a key point to be stressed. The necessity of excellent legal drafting and fool proof presentation leads to substantial gains in public interests is playing spoilers. The learning points given by author provide excellent direction to guide the relatively simple discussion.

Learning Points

1. Despite odds, there are things which could be done.
2. Homework and research is painstaking but definitely rewarding. Once certain documents are 'there', nobody can argue or deny the facts.
3. It is always rewarding to have a multi-pronged attack on any issue than one-by-one conflict. The three pronged simultaneous attack dissipated the energy and legal skills of the Company in this case.
4. Thorough knowledge of the "process" is very essential in government. Sometimes, process becomes more important than the goals and hence lot of patience is required.
5. Doggedly following up matters of importance is vital. Eyes have to be kept open for manipulation at any level.
6. Do not expect everything to go in your way. Even if the government succumbs to the might of the industrialist, there is consolation that the encroachment had been caught back and RR dues of Rs. 68 lakhs was paid up. Two out of three is not bad. And we never know whether we might even get two out of three.
7. The Assistant Collector had a security of tenure and some shield of protection. I was the only person in the District assured of one year stint ! This may not always be the case. So be prepared to leave things mid-way and not feel bad.

8. Personnal connections/contacts/friends in other services definitely help. Without this often the speed and success is never achieved.
9. Informal and personal sources and contacts are fast and reliable than government sources. Things that sound difficult within may be easy outside and *vice versa.*
10. While sending a report or submitting a line of argument, do not base your arguments on just one point, buttress it from all sides because you never know whether you get a second chance. Put the maximum on paper.
11. Never let others to guess your next move in a delicate situation. The best way is to avoid the possibility of a next move, i.e. As far as possible make it a one-move job. All the collected evidence/researched data can be fired at one go, and never in instalments. And all should be on paper.
12. When RTI applications come on delicate things on which you might be pressurized, proactively provide the documents, not waiting for the 30 days to lapse. It helps. In this case, Asianet had applied and we had given all data immediately. Though an MP was found on the TV abusing my Collector, nothing could be done that could damage or undo our work.
13. There are things that could be done. There are things that cannot be done. We are often not wise enough to distinguish between them. Political decisions are beyond our control and there is no necessity to try and control it either. Our work is to be done at our level, leaving the court open for other players who need to be acknowledged; we just need to record our position, especially on paper so as to influence other players and leave it at that.

TEACHING NOTE NO. 6
(7. Entebbe and Kandahar)

Time: 4 Hours (2 hours film's)

Methodology

It is ideal to show 'Operations Thunderbolt' film (available in internet) by Eyal Sher on Entebbe Hijack and then discuss the salient features of that classic commando operation. The aspects of negotiation, planning and leadership need to be focused on. It can then be contrasted against IC 814 efforts of India and contrasts can be drawn. Differentiating features of Israel's hard approach and India's soft stance (the soft State argument) can be examined. The Hijack doctrines of both countries and legal provisions can be analysed for effectiveness. How the doctrines have affected preparation or controlled terrorist onslaught could be examined in detail.

In the last 50 minutes the IC 814 film (National Geographic) can be shown and conclusions given in the last 10 minutes. Overall this case emphasize the need to strengthen doctrine in pressure tactics in matters of national policy and the capabilities State needs to build to tackle the growing menace of terrorist doctrines of various persuasions in our policy and neighbourhood.

The Central theme of the case is to examine the crucial role of leadership in Crisis decision-making. The leadership failure in Kandahar is contrasted with the importance of leadership proving to be an effective force multiplier in the Entebbe example. The case must be treated as an examination of the managerial and policy issues involved than detailing of military hardware and specifics of tactical planning.

The case discussion can be started by asking the participants to define the key features of Israel's approach to hostage taking and distinguish it with India's extant policy. There will be a tendency to depreciate India's approach especially in the context of Kandahar and Rubayya Saeed kidnap episodes. This must be balanced quite easily. Voices that bring in ethical dilemmas involved, i.e. whether 200 innocent lives are less worthy as against three criminals must be introduced. At his stage some participants will adopt hawkish hard postures. Examining the fallout of hard posturing by pointing out dire consequences of a botched attempt as in the Moscow Theatre siege must be pointed out. It may be pointed that Entebbe, though a 'model' rescue operation is 'one of its kind' and even Israel has not been able to reattempt it successfully.

The key role of negotiation as process and diversionary tactic may be impressed upon. The issues in mandate, operational styles, and distinction from military approaches must be made clear. The fact that force option must not be lost sight of at any stage of handling the crisis may be emphasised.

Roles laid down have been devised for junior functionaries (elsewhere in this issue) and executed using VHF/Telephones, etc. But the discussion will bring most of the issues which need be highlighted.

The learning points are: Need to wed a swift decision making process with well devised doctrine and tactical assets may be a befitting finale. Need to strengthen the far-reach of swift military extraction capability and the support of commandos, etc., may be made as pointers in the end.

A balance between the mindless criticism of State policy and arriving at pragmatic action points for future could be stressed. If experienced participants are there especially from the Armed Forces or internal security apparatus their specific experiences can be sought at appropriate points.

TEACHING NOTE NO. 7
(8. Dalit Inclusion)

Time: 2 Hours
Circulation Time: 7 days in advance.

This case explores the difficult modalities of ensuing *Dalit* representation in three Panchayats in Madurai, Tamil Nadu. Awarded the 'best social science case based paper' in 2009, by the International Development Research Centre (IDRC), Canada, and presented to the Institute of Social Science, Hague the case is developed on the field reports given by an IAS probationer on district training (Dr. Darez Ahamed).

A start can be made by exploring the pattern of crime against SCs in Tamil Nadu and Madurai from Table 10.1. The temporal variation of crime (reduction in PC Act crime and increase in POA crime) can be related to the overall spurt and control of anti SC crime in the late 1990s. The contribution of Local Governments and empowered communities in exposing and controlling anti SC crime can be explored.

Participants are likely to point out that in some parts minority and forward communities are also dominated upon. The reason and rationale for special protection for SCs stem from lack of representation and historical disempowerment. The vocational or economic deprivation of recent origin which is not associated with social exclusion must not be mixed up with socially imposed exclusion driven disempowerment.

The highlight of the case in the discussions on the site specific action strategy of the district administration. The dynamics of the mobilization achieved within the power structure of both communities (Kallar and SCs) the use of development as a counter weight to divisive issues and the role of media, political parties and civil society groups can be stripped.

Participants are likely to bring forth issues of corruption and mal-governance by some *dalit* leadership the overall desirability of caste based empowerment and the deleterious impact on society if separate constituencies were allowed as a result of Poona Pact negotiations. These should be examined in detail.

These are essentially mentioned not as articles of faith but provocateurs for exploring the counter factuals. The facilitator must position himself left of the centre politically for sparking genuine debate on the future of local self government and the empowerment of *dalits*.

The Idea of justice as fairness can be introduced as a concluding thought and ideas of viewing 'development' as a set of capacities in a democracy can be introduced. The possibilities open for a young civil servant in furthering the cause of the down trodden can be fitting conclusion. So that trainees as inspired to take up work in this crucial sector of State action without biases and full recognition that *dalit* empowerment and capacitation to work as full members of society, economy and polity is not an act of charity. It is a process Government cannot side step at all.

TEACHING NOTE NO. 8

(10. Innovations in Coastal Rural Water Supply)

Time: 1 Hour
Participations: 50

This is a relatively straight forward 'best practice case' which details the cost effective innovations an NGO is piloting in Kadalundi Grama Panchayat, Calicut, Kerala, to address the specific water quality problems affecting its inhabitants the NGO's team is wedding science and traditional practice. The NGO later picked up a World Bank innovation in 'development practice' award in India titled 'Development Market Place 2005'.

The focus is to emphasize that local low lost solutions are always available and an unfortunately overlooked in the mad rush for gunshot solutions and quick fixes. The process approaches, technology testing at local households and sustainable from local people are other defining features in this case. The facilitator must have good familiarity of the drinking water sector and especially water quality problems especially in saline areas for handling this case effectively. The need for lateral thinking and working with promising solution oriented agencies may be emphasized in conclusion.

TEACHING NOTE NO. 12

(Entebbe Game)

Time: 2 Hours

This simulation exercise is placed by 20 participants with role identity and wireless/Telephonic connectivity between the groups. This exercise styled after the Kandahar Hijack drama was a by product of the earlier related case developed by LDM, LBSNAA. Repeatedly used in the joint-civil Military Course run for officers of Civil and Military senior leaders, the case brings forth the centrality of leadership in managing sudden outset emergencies and the skill required to meet them. Negotiation skills and leadership ability can be tested by skilled facilitator. We recommend experienced facilitation from Centre for Disaster Management, LBSNAA, for initially running this case exercise.

Index